# Unorthodoxy

*A contrarian marketer's philosophy for*
*surviving the dying internet*

*Unorthodoxy:*
*A contrarian marketer's philosophy for*
*surviving the dying internet*

Copyright © 2024 Gil Gildner.
www.gilgildner.com

ISBN 978-1-7337948-6-2

Published by Baltika Press.

Printed in the United States of America.

GIL GILDNER

# UNORTHODOXY

**Reviews for *Building A Successful Micro-Agency* and *Becoming A Digital Marketer***

"Two marketers who know their subject well, and have the hands-on experience in the still-wild west of online marketing to know what works. They know what levers to pull."

— *Gary Bengier, CFO of eBay*

"The revolution of "stability over scaling" has begun, and Gil & Anya are leading the pack."

— *Kirk Williams, founder of ZATO*

"Great content, and really well-written."

— *Rand Fishkin, founder of Moz*

"Disregards an entire academic and professional Marketing *[sic]* community. This Verbose *[sic]* jargon that the authors mention referring to the American Marketing Association's definition of marketing is a synthesis of the complex scope of this discipline."

— *anonymous Amazon reviewer*

"A very boring read and I tried really hard to finish it but I couldn't."

— *Milly, Amazon reviewer*

"The first half of the book ain't detailed and I can understand why."

*— Mak, Goodreads reviewer*

"Totally lacking in any substantive information. A waste of time and money."

*— Chris, Amazon reviewer*

"It was okay. You're gonna need a lot more than this book."

*— M Earl Pulliam II, Amazon reviewer*

# Table of Contents

# Introduction

In *Unorthodoxy*, I am going to tie together a few thoughts that may seem totally disconnected from sales, marketing, business, or modern life in general. My thoughts are often a knotted mess, but the threads do—eventually—lead to the same end.

Here are a few things I believe to be true:

First, humans are not actually creative. We can only combine old things in new ways. As a wise man once said, humans can't invent new forms or ideas out of nothing; instead, we remix, recombine, or reinterpret what already exists. If that sounds misanthropic, wait until you read the rest of the book.

Second, evenly distributed bell curves do not practically exist in real life. Whether you're trying to quantify money, skills, morality, advertising, or agreeableness, thinking of things in terms of "averages" is incredibly misleading. As it turns out, going just a bit off the beaten path can bring massive results.

And third, the internet is dying. To be more specific, the original distributed and decentralized internet is gone, and a new monolithic centralized platform is taking its place. This is changing how we effectively market and sell to our audiences.

Creativity and bell curves and a dead internet: how do these tie into becoming a better advertising executive, salesman, stock trader, media buyer, ditch digger, real estate investor, fighter pilot, or Google Ads expert? I promise there's method behind this madness.

I should make it clear that I have nothing against *orthodoxy*. It serves most people moderately well (one might even say "averagely" well). But I have been fortunate enough to be able to see the flip side of an orthodox, mainstream, cookie-cutter approach to sales, marketing, and business.

I co-founded a boutique digital advertising agency almost eight years ago. Often marketing and advertising agencies are built by people coming from other agencies, but we were fortunate in not bringing any of that operating baggage along (best practices are often *worst* practices).

True to its name, Discosloth works on a truly unorthodox model: we're small, casual, flexible, hyper-focused, and slightly unprofessional. We have never had more than four team members.

Yet even with a small team, several of our clients have revenue in the billions, ad spend in the millions, and employee counts in the thousands. Discosloth goes on an annual international retreat (usually somewhere on the Mediterranean); every year we've maintained a net profit margin north of 70%; and literally all we do is digital advertising (you know, Google Ads and YouTube pre-roll and stuff like that). It's worked out pretty well. Despite all of that, the entire team has a pretty balanced life. I'm writing this from a coffeehouse right now, where I do half of my daily work every morning.

We have found success not by doing a full one-eighty in the opposite direction: we just figure out what the end goal is, and find the most direct and sustainable path. For instance, we decided early on we weren't going to do any cold-calling or hard-sales for our lead generation efforts: we were just going to build a brand by publishing the most insightful and detailed information possible (both online and in print). We were fortunate in our first book, *Becoming A Digital Marketer*, becoming an Amazon bestseller. It's since sold over 10,000 copies, prompting us to follow it up with *Building A Successful Micro-Agency* and maintaining a constant barrage of opinionated tweets.

And somehow, despite all the unorthodox ways in which we run our agency, our approach to weirdness has driven an entire business of managing tens of millions of dollars in digital advertising.

All that to say, I have nothing against *orthodoxy*.

People tend to gravitate towards what works. Whether in marketing, or in sales, or in life in general, the normal approach to any one problem is (more often than not) very likely the safest way to solve it. That's why most moderate, average, run-of-the-mill, normal businesses or freelancers or agencies or ecommerce stores tend to follow moderate, average, run-of-the-mill, normal paths.

Yet from time to time, things start breaking. Things start changing.

Sometimes you need to be *just ahead* of that change to take full advantage of it. Sometimes you need to steer *just off* the current course.

And if you want to take outsized risks (required in order to achieve outsized results) you will likely need to avoid orthodoxy altogether.

Call it *contrarianism*, call it *stupidity*, or perhaps just call it being too damn weird for the normal approach to make any sense, but I have found that trying to take an unorthodox perspective on just about anything has served me well.

At the end of the day, marketing is sales. And sales is marketing. You're trying to sell something. And part of selling something is getting the attention of the right person.

There are safe & reliable ways to do that, and then there are eye-opening wildly successful bizarre approaches to doing that. Truth be told, I'm interested in a bit of both.

I have structured this book in three sections.

Section 1 is about *being weird*: how the unorthodox mind works. It's about how difficult it is to actually be different. It's about how a massive gulf separates the "experts" from the "tyranny of the masses", and how no one is really actually in the middle of the bell curve. It's about ignoring best practices for the sake of best practices. It's about how those who aren't afraid to be a little out-of-the-ordinary end up reaping out-of-the-ordinary rewards.

Section 2 is about *the dying internet*: how the formerly decentralized internet has now coalesced into centralized, platform-centric channels. This influences how we approach marketing and sales. Now that everybody is on the internet, we have to double down on our own odd niches and stop worrying about trying to reach everybody. You have to take control of your brand, take control of your story, and focus on growing what you already have.

Section 3 is about *unorthodox sales and marketing*: how it's better to build brands, develop authority and influence within your industry, and take a long-term approach to tactics rather than short-term.

This book isn't tactical: I'm not going to teach anybody an exact recipe on how to build a brand and start making waves with your business. I decided to take this approach because, first of all, in the digital world the tactics change every single year. And second, I've found that the people who really get it don't really need to learn the tactics: they usually figure them out for themselves. Sometimes you just need a little poke to challenge your assumptions and start thinking about things differently. Think of this book as less of a manual, and more like a cattle prod.

Think of *unorthodoxy* as picking the Rogue as your character sheet during a game of Dungeons and Dragons.

I don't know if I could universally recommend picking the Rogue — unless you are prepared for a lifetime of slow starts, fairly consistent rejection, a likely string of failures, and perhaps a little bit of wandering in the woods.

However (and this is a big *however*) if you're looking to have a whole lot of fun, see the world, sell a lot of widgets, meet interesting people, run really memorable and successful ad campaigns, and maybe strike a few big wins, now's the time to flip some tables.

# Section 1: A Contrarian Mind

# Chapter 1: What Does It Mean To Be A Contrarian?

It was probably somewhere in Africa — broke, mid-twenties, camera in hand, a simmering unpleasantness boiling at the bottom of my stomach — that I realized I wasn't exactly trekking down the path most followed.

Most of my college classmates had gone on to be classically productive members of society, getting normal nine-to-five jobs in marketing or software sales or project management, and unlike myself they probably had dental insurance and a reliable car.[1]

Yet here I was, dodging the intermittent sub-Saharan rain showers, waiting on the side of the road for a motorcycle to come along so I could pay a few shillings for a ride into Kampala to pick up another gig shooting fundraising videos for one of the dozens of nonprofits scattered across Uganda.

For around five years after college, I went to dozens of countries across the world shooting photos, building websites, filming videos,

---

[1] *I drove a diesel 1984 Mercedes-Benz until 2014. I have never had dental insurance.*

bribing border guards, avoiding hawkers, getting pickpocketed, standing in mud, seeing some of the world's worst slums and talking with some of the world's worst people, and then seeing some of the world's most stunning locales and talking with some of the world's best people. I wish I could say, retroactively, that I had some sort of a vision. I wish I could lay out my detailed plan for industry domination. I wish I could truthfully say I knew exactly what I was doing.

I had no clue what I was doing. I was just *doing*.

Fortunately (most people would say *unfortunately*) being a bit different seems naturally ingrained for many folks.

As it turns out, the seldom-trod path I took in my twenties did end up at a very nice place in my thirties, but to say there was any sort of strategy behind it would be revisionism at its finest.

But I wouldn't change it for the world.

As a matter of fact, I've spent years in retroactive analysis, asking the simple question: "what exactly happened?" And although there's still a lot to dig out from my path seldom trod, I think I've come to some satisfactory conclusions.

Being a contrarian for the sake of being a contrarian is actually no different than following the herd blindly; you're just following a smaller, crankier herd.

A blanket distrust of common wisdom doesn't do anything for anyone. It's like the classic question posed by a mother to her easily influenced child: "if everyone else was jumping off a cliff, would you do it too?"

But most people *don't* jump off cliffs. Perhaps another equally insightful question should be: "so why *aren't* people jumping off cliffs?"

Taking a trajectory one hundred and eighty degrees from the herd can indeed bring huge returns, but only if there is actual wisdom behind it. Otherwise you're just being boneheaded for the sake of being boneheaded, and you'll probably end up far worse off than the herd.

Often you'll hear about famous money people who are called "contrarian investors". This is a common term to describe people who buy when prices are low, and sell when prices are high (and by the laws of supply & demand, low prices happen to be when most people are selling, and high prices happen to be when most people are buying). But calling these folks "contrarians" is actually a misnomer. I think the word people are looking for is *skeptic* rather than *contrarian*.

The word skeptic in this case implies that some level of searching, pondering, and analysis is taking place: someone who doesn't just take what they're told at face value, but instead digs into some research to make a decision for themselves.

Skepticism was simmering close to the surface for a while, but I became a convert back, once again, in Africa. It has been several years since I've trusted *anything* I see reported in the media — *anything*. And I have real reason behind this.

In September and October 2014 I was in Liberia during the Ebola outbreak. I was staying in the compound shared by two humanitarian organizations, Doctors Without Borders and Samaritan's Purse. I stayed in Dr Fankhauser's house[2] and I photographed and videoed day in, day out, driving a crappy Mitsubishi Pajero around town.

The feeling in the capitol city of Monrovia was bizarre. No one shook hands. Everyone dipped the soles of their shoes into pans of bleach before entering doorways. Driving around, I was shaken down for bribes by police, and offered bribes to other guards to take photos. Most of this was stuff I'd had to do before in other countries, but this time the streets were dead quiet (very different from the chaos I was used to in Western Africa).

On October 2nd (which happened to be my birthday) I woke up to Dr Fankhauser telling me to suit up in a hazmat suit and go into the Ebola unit itself, an old church that had been converted into a 78-bed unit. After orderlies suited me up, duct taped the seams, double-suited me, and made sure the goggles and mask and hood were also taped up, I took a GoPro in. I still have the nearly two-hour footage of the experience. In the interest of tastefulness I will leave out the most graphic details, but near the end of my hours inside I

---

[2] *Later Dr Fankhauser was named one of Time Magazine's Persons of the Year*

was helping Dr Brown[3] by shining a flashlight onto a lady while he stabbed her with an adrenaline syringe. I've never been a queasy sort of person, in general, but I was *hot*. Encased in the hazmat suit, sweat literally filling up the bottom of my goggles, I was nearly sent over the edge. I was going to pass out. I motioned to Dr Brown that I was nauseous. He pointed to the door and said "get out!" Nurses stripped me out of the suit, layer by layer, spraying me down with bleach. I stood in my underwear in the fresh air of the courtyard, stomach returning to normal. I dunked the GoPro in bleach and let it sit for a few minutes.

And this is where the distrust in media comes into play. As frightening as Ebola was, it is only spread by direct contact with bodily fluids. In Liberia, it spread fast. But it was entirely cultural. Liberians observe a practice of embracing the dead (a ritual where the whole family would sleep in the same room as the body for several days after death). Ebola had a zero percent chance of affecting most of the world — at least anywhere with a modern understanding of health and hygiene. Back home in Arkansas, we don't sleep with the dead.

So there I was, fresh out of the Ebola unit, and a Sky News team from Britain is set up just outside the unit. There were three journalists in a Land Rover. Here's the kicker: the reporter was wearing a hazmat suit, a mask, and goggles. But hardly 18 inches

---

[3] *Dr Brown even made it to the cover of Time Magazine (unfortunately, not my photo)*

away, both the cameraman and the producer were in flip-flops and shorts. It was all smoke & mirrors. The Sky News footage, which I saw later, was as dramatized as possible...with the viewers never realizing that behind the camera, all was normal, and there was no actual reason to wear personal protective equipment outside of the Ebola unit itself.

I went to bed with a racing mind.

Then, I woke up at midnight, Liberia time, to dozens of messages and a missed call from my mother. I'd been on the six o'clock news, and my grandparents (who hadn't been told I was spending a couple weeks in Liberia, for obvious reasons) called my mom asking "just why Gil had Ebola?"

An ABC reporter had written the most factually incorrect and technically deceiving story imaginable, and it had run on the local news. They didn't even have actual footage, hadn't asked me for an interview or comments, anything: they'd just found an outdated Facebook profile photo to use and run with it. It got my job wrong, implied that I was bringing Ebola back home to Arkansas, and had even gotten opinions from local doctors without even telling them the real details.

Among the dozens of messages were frantic diatribes from strangers telling me "they'd follow me around town wiping off every doorknob I touched, so their kids wouldn't die" and "let the Africans take care of themselves" and "who do I think I am?"[4]

*(To be fair, after cussing out the director of the local ABC affiliate and threatening libel suit, he took the story off the internet).*

But that didn't stop the paranoia. Flying back (I had to go through CDC testing in Atlanta) I heard that the same news station had a crew at the airport waiting to ambush me when I arrived. So my father met me, snuck me downstairs through a back elevator, and brought a bag of groceries to my apartment to last through self-imposed quarantine.

It was all ridiculous, honestly.

Whenever you see someone on camera wearing a hazmat suit, I guarantee you, behind the camera is a guy in flip-flops.

How does this relate to contrarianism?

Here's how the public reaction to something like Ebola was structured: the ignorant masses were in total fear. The total contrarians said it was absolute bunk. And the critical skeptics knew it was most a very real thing, but that it was also not something anyone needed to freak out about.

Now, it's not that Ebola wasn't a big deal. It was.

But as I mentioned before, Ebola could *never have spread in the United States,* or for that matter in any part of the developed world. It

---

[4] *I thought I was single. Two weeks earlier, while on another project in Costa Rica, I got a call from the boss of the organization I freelanced for. He said, and I quote, "You're single right? Everybody else here has a family and doesn't want to go."*

is spread by direct and continued contact with bodily fluids. It was quite a big deal in Liberia, but (thankfully) the vast majority of the world does not embrace the bodies of their dead.

It is easy to embrace, instead, total fear. Stoked by the yellow journalism of a dying newspaper and television news industry, the "masses" will of course begin to fear.

And the contrarians, seeing the fear, take the extreme opposite view. But this isn't entirely accurate either, because it's not like Ebola was fake. It was very real, very frightening disease. I have seen the bodies.

But the reality (the facts we saw play out in real life) is that Ebola was actually not a pandemic, but a super-localized epidemic. For as terrible a disease as it was, and in such non-hygienic conditions as it erupted in, it was contained fairly quickly. The developed world had absolutely nothing to fear.

The skeptic should always look at things critically. In this case, realize that it was a very alarming disease, but also come to peace with the fact that it is very easy to avoid contracting the disease at all.

Let's illustrate this in marketing terms. Say that some sort of product is trending, advertisers are advertising, companies are producing, and investors are piling on: an anti-aging cream that promises eternal youthful looks, for example. A pure contrarian sees this product and refuses to enter this market. *("It's a scam! no cream is actually magic!")*

But a critical skeptic sees this product, is immediately doubtful, and investigates. Perhaps he does indeed find that it's entirely hype. But perhaps the skeptic finds that the idea itself may actually have *something* going for it. If anything, it shows a demand for things that help you age less dramatically. Perhaps this particular anti-aging cream is a trend that will die out: but what if there were other actually-real products which actually *did* help moisturize the skin and prevent wrinkles?

The pure contrarian could miss out on some of the most obvious plays in history, while the skeptic has the best of both worlds: paranoid enough to pass on bubbles and scams, but open-minded enough to recognize when the herd is heading in the right direction.

The real power is when you're just *very slightly off track*. You're just outside the mainstream to be able to look at it from an elevated height, but not far enough away that you're in outer space, and all you can see is a blue dot.

When everybody else is heading 12 o'clock, you don't want to default to 6 o'clock. That just looks like you're boneheaded.

What's far more powerful is the ability to adjust your heading to 1 o'clock.

Say that everyone is buying Acme Oil when the gold price is going up. The skeptic within you looks at the greater macroeconomic situation, and you agree that the prognosis looks good for oil. An actual contrarian — someone boneheaded for the sake of being boneheaded — won't buy anything related to oil at all. Maybe they'll just buy an EV stock.

A clever skeptic will instead find something *tangential*, perhaps a smaller midstream energy company which is overlooked by most of the investing herd, but still stands to profit significantly from Acme Oil's success. So they find something that hasn't been piled on by institutional investors, and this gives them a bit more leverage than the huge exchange-traded funds that go for the tried & true.

Similarly, a clever digital marketer will not eschew old-school traditional marketing altogether, but perhaps realize that billboards are an overlooked marketing opportunity with surprisingly affordable monthly costs.[5]

And a clever sales guy won't come up with an entirely new form of sales, but instead find some hidden niche markets in which to develop relationships.

Right now, we're in a state of change when it comes to the internet. Earlier I stated that the internet was dying, but that was a bit facetious. It's actually just in a state of major rebirth.

The problem is that I'm not sure if the change is positive. I'll get more into this later, but the internet is in the process of shifting from a distributed, diverse, creative, and decentralized model into a platform-based, centralized, consumer model.

The barrier to entry for success has gone haywire. The "long tail"

---

[5] *I recently inquired about the costs of renting a billboard along the busiest section of the interstate in my region. It costs around $750 per month.*

is dead. Advertising is now far more expensive. Organic traffic has plummeted. We are no longer competing with millions, we are competing with billions. It is because we are no longer a grain of sand in a bucket: we're a grain of sand on a very long beach.

The pure contrarian may see this try to abandon the internet altogether. But I think the clever skeptic will just find his particular angle to take advantage of this new development.

---

## Chapter 1 Summary

*Today's world is massively interconnected. That means that the only way to stand out is by being different. But when you have eight billion competing people out there, that's really hard for a brand to do, especially in marketing where everyone prides themselves in "thinking differently". Critical thinking is the only thing that will really, truly, get you and your brand in a better place, because very few people seem to be able to take a step back, develop their self-awareness, and think for themselves.*

# Chapter 2: Thinking Like A Weirdo

If you've ever watched a classic coming-of-age movie from the 1980s or 1990s, perhaps a John Hughes film like *The Breakfast Club* or *Ferris Bueller's Day Off* or *Sixteen Candles*, you'll be familiar with the idea of the "jock" and the "nerd" archetypes.

These stereotypical characters are inspired by real-life patterns (as are all stereotypes) and obviously make for good cinema. But I didn't realize until later in my life just how much these stereotypes had influenced my idea of how the world works.

I went through college with a bias against jocks. In retrospect, I had a built-in assumption that if you were athletic and looked good and were popular and wore preppy clothes and were going for a business degree, you were likely a dumb jerk. It's not that this can't happen — it often *does* — but because I was a nerd, the idea that everybody who was bigger, stronger, better looking, and more sharply dressed was something I embraced for entirely the wrong reasons.

I was looking at the surface, without considering what it takes under the surface in order to become that person. As it turns out, a lot of those dumb jocks had the discipline to train physically, the charisma to be popular, the foresight to go for lucrative degrees, and the ability to work well with a team.

Ironically, a lot of the smart hipsters I surrounded myself with ended up dead broke in aspirational creative roles, or stuck in a paper-pushing dead-end local government office job. The jocks ended up on Wall Street or Silicon Valley. *(Some of them did peak in college, as is the stereotype, but fewer than you'd think).*

What I learned from this is that thinking differently is harder than it looks. Although I was the disheveled hipster who probably looked like he thought differently, I actually wasn't. I was just as susceptible to groupthink as anyone else, it just happened my group was a little smaller. It took a while to realize that thinking differently is actually just self-awareness.

You'll always be in a group. You'll always have affinities and biases. You shouldn't even necessarily reject these. It's far better to just be self-aware of your positioning, and select better positions if needed.

If you're actually going to be original, you have to take a step back. Look at yourself (and your behavior and viewpoints) from a distanced perspective, as if you're having an out-of-body experience, and decide if you like what you see.

Yet weirdness isn't static. It changes, because culture is constantly cycling. What once was weird becomes normal, and what was once normal becomes strange. There is a constant back-and-forth struggle between the button-ups and the graphic tees, between rap and classical, between poor and rich, between cars and trucks. Thinking differently from the herd requires a constant shift: it's not something you can just figure out once and for all.[6]

During the tumultuous American presidential election cycle of 2024, the only thing that astute observers universally agreed on was that the PR machine was charging ahead at full steam. At the snap of a finger, entire swathes of each party would switch up the rhetoric, displaying an impressive front in a unified memetic movement.

For instance, during a few crucial weeks a few months before the election, a wave of carefully crafted denunciations against the vice presidential candidate issued forth from the opposing party (as is to be expected). What surprised me, though, is that the opposition chose the word *weird* as their primary epithet.

I'm sure this word was heavily workshopped. The army of consultants and market researchers and advisory boards and campaign intern affinity groups probably paid a pretty penny to test this word. Within the matter of a couple days, everyone (from Vice Presidents to Senators to Congressmen to the endless pundits and wannabe political influencers scattered across the internet) was calling the new vice presidential nominee *weird*.

As it turns out, the vice presidential candidate embraced the insult, retweeting things like "he is weird" which if anything cemented his weird underdog reputation.

---

[6] *In the early 1990s, listening to Cypress Hill or My Bloody Valentine would have been edgy. Now, it's probably edgier to listen to Liszt or Mozart.*

Which brings me to the point: weirdness is not necessarily equivalent to badness. Weirdness is simply the antonym of normality, and if people aren't super happy with the current state of normality, then of course they'll embrace weirdness.

For many, many years, nerds were weird. Nerds eventually went from being mercilessly bullied in every 80's movie, to being the absolute most richest and powerful in the world, but for many years they were the underdogs. They hadn't made their money yet. They hadn't changed the world.

The lifecycle of the weirdo went like this: first they were weird nerds, and they got bullied at school because they weren't normal. Then, they actually did something that mattered and they made a lot of money, and for a brief instant they became normal. Then, because they were actually so incredibly successful and powerful, they became weird again. The only difference is that now they have billions of dollars and jet to fly to their private bunker, so they probably don't care as much.

The hard part about being a weirdo is the first part of the cycle: being weird *before* you've become successful. And by definition, weirdness is not successful at first. If you are going to think differently, you'll be thinking differently in a bizarre niche which is not classically lucrative or influential. Otherwise, everyone would be doing it.

You also have to be weird in the right ways, not the wrong ways.

Some folks are just weird, in an anti-social and relationally bombastic way, which is just a character flaw. You need to be normal in a human manner. You must be fine with thinking strategically and conceptually in a truly bizarre manner, but still be tolerable to be around.

Tying weirdness back to contrarianism, the mere act of thinking differently isn't as much about being weird for the sake of weirdness, as much as being okay with not aligning for the sake of alignment. A contrarian who just takes the opposite viewpoint for the sake of being different is just a jackass. A weird person who chooses weirdness just to not be normal is also a jackass, except he's likely extremely self-absorbed and anti-social.

It's more about resisting the siren call of mindless orthodoxy, mainstream alignment, pop culture, and societal assumptions. Rather than just listening to the world's most popular music artist simply because it's the world's most popular music artist, why not listen to whatever you actually want to listen to? It may seem overly simplistic and perhaps a bit unimportant, but the impetus behind consumption is often an indicator of what the person is looking for.

Often, it's an absence of impetus which is actually the main driver of behavior. A "normal" person may actually just be consuming "normal" things because it does not require any effort whatsoever. And I suspect this laziness lays behind a lot of the worst elements of our society (I am guilty of it in my consumption as well). This is why things feel cookie-cutter. If you've ever seen an American neighborhood in which all the houses look the same, all the chain restaurants are identical clones, everyone drives same-looking cars to similar-functioning jobs, and every night everyone watches the same reality shows on the same brand television screens, this is because it is very simply the lowest effort possible.

The human drive behind this lifestyle is actually universal. It's easy to make fun of the American approach as delineated above, but that's because it's probably the most popular due to the saturation of American media. It's actually everywhere. Fly into a dirt airfield in innermost Africa, and there are millions of people behaving just like everyone else around them. Pull into a town in the middle of Germany, and you'll be surrounded by people living identically to everyone around them.

This isn't necessarily even a critique. It's an observation, and being self-aware of our tendency towards orthodoxy is an important step in figuring out what it actually takes to be weird — *good* weird.

## Chapter 2 Summary

*One of the most fascinating things about working in marketing is that you get to work with companies with such a variety of people types, mentalities, maturity levels, profitability, ambitions, cultures, and vibes. The term "weirdness" could almost be described as "not caring what people think" which is actually a massively effective way to run a business. I like to say that I've never seen an insanely successful startup which has MBAs calling the shots. The wildest success stories are always companies owned by crazy guys who wear Crocs and collect black-market ancient Egyptian antiquities.*

# Chapter 3: The Bell Curve Fallacy

In this chapter I am going to hammer home a point which may seem, on the surface, to be trivial.

But so much of my approach to unorthodoxy centers around this point — that people are either *very clueless* or *very clued-in*, not anything in between — that the bell curve fallacy is hard to ignore.

Most people think of most real-world results as evenly distributed across a gentle bell curve. If you were ever forced to undergo the drivel that makes up most psychology classes in university, you probably saw a lot of these graphs.

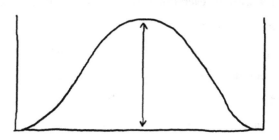

*This is a normal distribution, also called a symmetrical probability distribution.*

This is simplistic. It is not actually how results are distributed in real life, simply and evenly distributed across a bell curve. I don't think most people are positioned at the 50th percentile — they are usually closer to the 1st percentile (nothing) or the 99th percentile (everything). They either know *everything about something* or they know *nothing about something.* They either care a lot or they don't care at all.

To put it simply, people are either really good or really bad at things. We like to envision humans as a big lump in the middle (a sort of 50th percentile blah) but it's actually far more complicated than that: there are a lot of local minima and local maxima.

Most people seems to assume that failure comes from risk. They also think that success comes from taking the safe route. This is why the "bell curve" approach (thinking that safety is in numbers, or that the proven route is the best route) is so comfortable for them.

In other words, cautious people (especially academic types) would prefer to have predictable, middle-of-the-road, benchmarked results. They assume everything is lumped together in the 50th percentile of mediocrity.

But it gets even more interesting. Many pursuits have a lower minimum, but not upper maximum. This is because many things have a hard cut-off at the bottom of whatever you're measuring.

For instance, the minimum distance you can throw a javelin is 0 meters. You can't throw it *less far* than zero. But there really isn't a maximum, is there? Every year, someone has the chance to break the record in javelin-throwing distance. You can always throw it a *little bit farther.*

You can apply this to measuring many things (*how much money can you make, how many items can you sell, how many ads can you run?*)

If you were to graph these sorts of things on a bell curve, it would not look like an even distribution, but instead be clumped near zero.

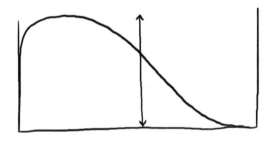

*Since most things have a hard cut-off at zero, this graph shows how skills and results are actually portrayed more often in reality.*

The default is to be inert. At rest. At zero.

So? How does this affect you: a marketer or advertiser or salesman or taxicab driver? It affects you because it means that a very little bit of effort provides outsized results. The results are exponential when it comes to moving yourself along that weighted curve.

Trying a little bit is more than most people will do. Trying *hard* is more than almost anybody will do. You can get yourself into the

90th percentile of any pursuit simply by doing *anything*, and likely put yourself into the 98th percentile by staying in the game and working a tiny bit harder.

What if the real successes—the 99th percentile results—come from *going all-in?*

This is the plague of iteration, safety, caution, and bell curve mentality.

Do you think Karl Benz could have iterated the automobile, and released a half-drivable concept to the public? Do you think Apple could have iterated the iPhone, and released a smartphone that only *sometimes* works?

If you have one shot to create outsized success, an iterative process is not the way to go.

An iterative workflow is often touted as the way to success, and it's definitely been the way many folks have built solid companies, but it's actually far less likely to succeed than the traditional way.

The traditional way? Coming up with a good idea and executing it well.

Here's why. Building a business is not the same as building software. You cannot iterate a restaurant in two-week sprints.

Sustaining business success through iteration is one thing, absolutely, but sprints are not the way to start most things from scratch.

I have worked with hundreds of small business founders over the past few years, and by this point I can sense the probability of success or failure within a few minutes of speaking to someone.

Many folks start a business without being all-in. They go halfway. In their mind, this hedged approach is safe because they're iterating. They're "just investing $5,000 and two months" to test the water, and stay in, *if it's safe*.

Over the years I have watched these folks do this a dozen times. Iterating, playing it safe, going halfway. That initial "$5,000 and two months" eventually turns into a half-hearted "$30,000 and a few years" of mediocrity. It rarely proceeds beyond that point.

It would have been better if they'd have just clenched their teeth and kicked ass with a single solid idea with great execution, funding, and follow-through. They should have had *skin in the game*.

I learned this the hard way, back in the day. For many years, while freelancing, I half-heartedly started a dozen projects. I subscribed to the "agile" idea of trying a million things and seeing which one sticks. I threw spaghetti at the wall like crazy. The problem is, if I didn't see any traction the first few weeks, I would assume there was no market, or it was a bad idea, or it just wasn't possible to see success in this field.

The real problem? I did not execute well, persevere long enough, or have enough faith in the idea. The agile, iterative approach did not allow me time to realize I was actually just doing things poorly. Because of this, I prematurely abandoned many good ideas back in 2008 (which would have been nice to still have around).

When starting our agency, if we'd based our judgement of Discosloth's future potential merely upon the first couple months of revenue, we would have shut down and pivoted far too soon. It took months of full-time work to see traction. Discosloth could not have been iterated.

It was all or nothing.

Here's why this anti-bell curve idea is so important: it doesn't take much work to get out of the "big lump" near zero. Simply *not being inert,* and doing *anything,* automatically gets you near the 90th percentile of success.

The real upper tail of success requires significant risk. This is the number one reason most companies failing at marketing and sales. They are afraid of risk.

Often, companies approach their business model with all of the charm and charisma of a pivot table. And that's it. It's just numbers, all of which are pored over by an MBA and compared to some sort of industry baseline or a Gartner report. This is the private equity approach to success, and I have not seen this approach build a decent brand.

This approach is the mathematical approach that will get you to the 50th percentile, but no more, no less.

Many businesses are so allergic to risk that they won't do anything that hasn't been done before. They won't approve any strategy which hasn't been proven by other companies.

Yet, paradoxically, they want results better than anybody else is getting.

---

## Chapter 3 Summary

*Achieving better results (breaking out of the bell curve of mediocrity) unavoidably require a dip into the risky unknown. Without fail, the most successful companies that we have worked with are okay with going all-in, even at significant risk. They understand that normal approaches bring normal results, so sometimes it's worth trying something absolutely new and unproven. They understand that action begets action.*

# Chapter 4: Heretics

Disruption.

I hate writing that word. It's been co-opted into business jargon. You know, like when folks talk about developing cross-functional teams with agile methodology and flat hierarchy.[7]

Being disruptive has become fashionable in tech, marketing, and the business world at large. The word's become watered down, though. It used to mean *let's flip these tables over*, and now it means *let's improve a process*.

Turning industries on their heads is much more exciting.

I don't think any industry is particularly sacrosanct.

Except, apparently, recipe bloggers.

I recently noticed a little furor developing within the micro-startup world. A pair of developers started a little service called Recipeasly.

You know how, when you're looking for recipes online, you have to read through someone's life story before you even get to the

---

[7] *Sentences like this are exactly why I quit my last job, the one right before Anya and I started Discosloth almost eight years ago.*

ingredients part? You've got to read a thousand-word story about the author's spring break trip to Barcelona where she glimpsed a dashing Spanish chef in the kitchen of a little cafe and was introduced to a spice she has since added to all of her tapas dishes, and later when she rescued a mangy old dog it turned out to be a purebred Spanish water dog previously owned by the prime minister of Andorra.

That's what this app was supposed to solve: stripping out all the fluff and displaying the essentials in an easy-to-read format.

I would love this service, and so would any other guy who happens to be standing in his kitchen with a knife in his hand.

Apparently, however, it was disruptive enough that food bloggers across the world erupted in fury. (Food bloggers, it might be said, who are dependent upon page views, page scrolls, sponsorships, and time on page for their income). How dare you simplify my 3,000 word essay on lasagna? How dare you make an easy-to-print version that saves five pages of paper? Those stories make the recipe *better!*

Over one thousand angry replies later, the developers announced they were taking the project down.

That's not the way to be disruptive! I would love to get thousands of bloggers riled up just because I launched a new web app. It would make me double down, a clear message that I'm obviously doing *something* right.

Is the food writing world so sacrosanct that we can't change it up? Is there some Demigod of Culinary Storytelling that we must placate? Is there an Archbishop of Narrative Cuisine who patrols the world of food bloggery?

It's not like Recipeasly would have shut down food blogs. Don't these bloggers own their own platform? There is an audience who *does* like to read about Janine's quaint family trip to a cabin in the Smokies where she discovered this sumptuous Appalachian Beef Chili recipe good for families of all sizes. They'll still have a life story audience.

It's sort of like reality TV, except it's a parmesan chicken recipe.

I just want to know how many onions to chop.


Heretics create change.

Whether it's Galileo insisting that we actually orbit the sun, or Martin Luther insisting that we don't need to pay the Pope cash in order to be forgiven, or Leif Ericsson insisting that there is land beyond the horizon, or Thoreau insisting that violent force is wrong, or Solzhenitsyn insisting that perhaps Stalinism isn't the best manifestation of Marxism — all of these heretics wrought lasting change, and left the world a better place.

I don't think any of us who fiddle around on the internet will ever be in Thoreau's orbit, but we don't even have the balls to disrupt our own little industries.

If you aren't pushing the boundaries, nothing's going to change.

Own a business? Push the limit to how much you can charge. Or undercut everyone else. Offer so much more than your competitors. Whatever!

Marketing a product? Make your offering impossible to compete with. Use branding that no one else would dare use.

Writing a book? Write things you believe in, even if they risk ostracizing yourself.[8]

Building your personal brand? Stop filtering your messaging to what you think people want to hear.

Creating an app to simplify recipes? Just do it. If it negatively affects a food blogger's traffic, maybe they'll start simplifying their own recipes, and by pushing boundaries you'll have enacted change. You can't try to disrupt, and then get cold feet the instant they push back.

Being a heretic is a lot of work. And that is why most people *aren't* heretics. They're orthodox.

Our civilization, as we have progressed towards an ambiguous perfection, has lost some of the dirt along the way.

I don't mean bad dirt. I mean *good* dirt.

Near total freedom and independence is almost impossible to achieve in an interconnected, bureaucratic, streamlined world. You really start to wonder if the Luddites saw something of an actual prophecy in the steam-powered machines they sabotaged.

There used to be a frontier. Wherever you were in the world, you could go just a little bit further and find total independence. You

---

[8] *In this book I have a chapter called "People Are Stupid…" which will probably get myself ostracized.*

might have had to raise your own cattle and shoot your own deer with a flintlock—maybe fend off a few wild bears, or die from diphtheria—but you would have been pretty damn free.

The value of this free state has been largely lost. My house, tied in to the electrical grid, fiber internet, and clean water spoils our desire for independence. I can't even drive down the interstate without Lane Assist telling me that I'm drifting towards the median. In a world where I can drive a 437 horsepower car that intelligently keeps me within the lines, I don't have much freedom. I'm highly dependent upon the system, the system that brought me the shackles that I happily adorn in order to live in air conditioning.

We've been suppressing urges that are buried deep within us: the urges that drove Alexander to the Far East, that drove Leif Eriksson to the shores of America, that drove men to build cabins in the uninhabited wilds and set foot on empty atolls — how does my air conditioning play into this?

There is a lost art of doing whatever you want — in the manner that gives you the most independence and freedom. The art of extending a middle finger while staying fully compliant. The art of developing a lifestyle that is entirely legitimate — legally, financially, morally — while still doing whatever the hell you want.

The art of being so good at what you do that the tepid fools over in the revenue department cower before your success. The art of adapting to the system so well that the assaults thrown against you by jealous cowards bounce off and melt like shaved ice.

I have not become this good at doing whatever the hell I want. But I do know that it's the closest thing a modern man can do in the pursuit of total freedom and independence, short of moving to a jungle in the middle of nowhere and living in a bamboo hut.

---

**Chapter 4 Summary**

*Most people don't actually want to be different, so as long as you are okay with being seen as weird, or heretical, or nonconformist, you have the ability to change the perception of your brand (whether that brand is you personally, or a company you are operating). It's hard to fake authenticity, even though many try. The truth always comes out. Are you actually, truly unorthodox?*

# Chapter 5: Underdogs Eventually Win

I tend to have a distaste for business books. The vast majority are either full of vapid aphorisms or ghostwritten by clueless writers (same goes for most marketing books, too, unfortunately).

Yet one book I always return to is *Zero To One* by Peter Thiel, one of the founders of PayPal in the late 1990s, and current multibillionaire. An entire section in the book dissects personalities of successful startup founders. This chapter opens with my favorite line:

*"Of the six people who started PayPal, four had built bombs in high school."*[9]

Maybe this just tickles my fancy because as a teenager I definitely never ever built any explosive devices from household materials, *ever,* but the line supports the classic underdog story: a skinny or overweight acne-pocked computer geek becomes software billionaire.

The world's richlist is currently peppered with nerds, strange creatures that would have been played by Anthony Michael Hall in those archetype-ridden John Hughes movies. Loners who hacked

---

[9] *Zero To One: Notes on Startups, or How to Build the Future, by Peter Thiel and Blake Masters, 2014.*

into mainframes, played Dungeons & Dragons, bullied by the football players, and definitely had something to prove.

This wave of nerdy underdog success lasted for several decades, but I think it began to subside around the time I entered the workforce. By then, everyone and their grandmother knew that *tech = money.*

What I'm really interested in learning is who comprises the next wave of underdogs.

In the 1980s through early 2000s, you could just get into software, not even be very good at it, and retire wealthy within a few years. It's been commoditized now.

There was a brief wave of this antihero success arc with cryptocurrency. It was the same story all over again: unpopular, social misfits becoming millionaires or billionaires within a few short years, all from adoption of an unproven and highly risky new idea. Until finally, when during the past few years, I couldn't go into a single bar or coffee shop without overhearing a bartender talk about investing in Dogecoin.

Crypto is becoming commoditized, now, and newly minted crypto-billionaires will be a little more rare going forward.

So who's next?

I have no earthly idea, to be honest. This book is just me coining new aphorisms and blabbing. It's not a prediction machine. But I do think I know a few things that will define the next wave, because they have defined previous waves of underdog successes.

First, there will be a universal disregard and (one might even say) outright disrespect for the new idea. Scholars and journalists love ragging on new ideas, until those new ideas turn out a few folks worth more than the GDP of small countries.

Second, it will be counter-cultural, and not in a cool way. How many up-tight, fully-suited Wall Street financiers passed on investing in early tech companies because the founders were wearing jeans and drove beater Hondas?

Third, it will be impossibly idealistic. PayPal's original company mission was to replace the US dollar (it didn't end up doing that, mostly because of regulatory pressure, but that was the original end goal).

Fourth, it will be risky. Getting into tech in the early days meant putting thousands of dollars into soon-obsolete computers, missing out on traditionally stable and lucrative careers in finance or law, and "getting lucky" in crypto meant putting thousands of dollars into a highly unproven new idea.

All of these factors work together to create something that becomes a huge, outsized success for a chosen few. The very reasons that the masses avoid new ideas (the disrespect, counter-culture, idealism, financial risk) become the reasons that the outliers who pierced the veil become so successful when it does take off.

These factors filter out the competition: the bottom of the bell curve.

And personally, knowing myself, I'd add in a fifth factor: I think

I'll be suspicious of this new wave, whenever and wherever it comes. This new wave will defy logic, and often my tendency is to look at things pragmatically rather than idealistically.

But I hope that I will be able to put my money where my mouth is, and be open to crazy and risky new ideas.

In the venture capital world (of which I am not a part, but I enjoy peeking into) there are tools used to classify, categorize, and compare potential startup investment opportunities. Some of these are public-facing, others are internal processes developed in-house on Sand Hill Road (the area of Silicon Valley famous for headquartering VC companies).

Many factors are used to sort out potential opportunities: looking at how profitable a startup is, how lean it runs, if the CEO knows how to code, if the founders have good track records, etc. But one of the most common factors is immigrant founders.

At first glance you might think that's just more politically correct nonsense.

*("Ah! A company founded by a proto-pescatarian Pacific Islander nonbinary skateboarding activist! We must invest!")*

But it's not just that.

Venture capital companies prefer to back immigrant-founded startups because they are more successful. End of story. The data is so wildly strong on this that it's not even up for debate. Over 43% of all tech startups in the US were founded by immigrants: and of all the unicorns in the US (startups valued over a billion dollars) a solid 55% of them were started by immigrants.

And it's not just startups, or *new* companies...of all the companies in the Fortune 500, a full 45% were started by either immigrants or their children.

As far as small business creation: every year from 1996 to 2016, there were twice as many small businesses started by immigrants than from native-born Americans.

Immigrants from a gamut of countries ranging from Australia, Russia, Switzerland, Ukraine, Germany, Cambodia, and Vietnam all have significantly higher household incomes than native-born Americans.

This isn't random correlation, to be sure. There is significant causation, and I think most notably it's because there's a significant hurdle to legal immigration. It's a pre-filter. You're going to get the highest-performing software developers, accountants, scientists, entertainers, and even tradesmen coming in to make serious moolah.

And frankly, I think a lot of it is simply *being different*.

It's often been said, and I believe it, that being born in the US is like winning the lottery. You can live your whole life, if so desired, barely lifting a finger. I know people my age who still haven't ever had a real job, and they somehow still enjoy the luxuries of life like Netflix, advanced education, new cars, hoppy beers and organic seltzer waters.

If one could have all this at one's fingertips, why would you really bother with the risk of starting something new? One could bemoan the state of the American entrepreneurial spirit, and there might be some truth in that.

But as long as we have underdogs building stuff, I think we'll be fine.

I have noticed a very specific behavioral trend in a handful of highly successful people who I've had the pleasure of meeting. Oddly enough, I first noticed this trend — almost a sort of tic — while watching Peter Thiel, the author of *Zero To One* mentioned earlier. I noticed that during interviews, when confronted with a statement of fact or opinion, Thiel does not necessarily argue with the statement. If he's uncertain about the statement, he simply pauses, thinks, and then asks a question that challenges the assumption of the statement.

I've seen this behavior replicated across friends and acquaintances (none of whom are quite as successful, perhaps, but all of whom are undoubtedly accomplished). Say something ill-informed or off-the-cuff, and they'll likely frown a little bit, pause, think, and then ask you a direct question which absolutely destroys your assumption.

One of Thiel's most famous contrarian ventures was the funding of a Roth IRA with just under $2,000 of startup stock shares in 1999.[10] A Roth IRA is tax-advantaged in that you pay tax on the money when you contribute, not when you withdraw. Fortunately

---

[10] *Lord of the Roths: How Tech Mogul Peter Thiel Turned a Retirement Account for the Middle Class Into a $5 Billion Tax-Free Piggy Bank, ProPublica, 2021.*

for Thiel, the shares went to the moon, and his IRA is now worth almost $6 billion. As long as he waits until 2027 to withdraw, he will have a nearly $6 billion at his fingertips without having to pay confiscatory taxes on it.

The skeptical approach isn't popular. It comes across as brusque or socially "off". You can find loads of haters, if you bring up Thiel's Roth strategy. But the thing to remember is that these truly revolutionary people aren't the *popular* ones. They're the *doers*, and people who get things done aren't always the most normal of all of us.

They're contrarians and underdogs in the best sense possible: people who don't take things for granted, people who challenge any assumption that they come across, pursue tactics or ideas that may not align perfectly with the zeitgeist, and aren't afraid to brush against the grain.

---

**Chapter 5 Summary**

*Often business owners, marketers, or advertisers fall into the "best practices" trap. They find themselves asking for proof, or trying to find industry benchmarks, or discovering previous success stories. But the reality is: if any crazily effective strategy has well-documented processes and case studies, it's probably not crazily effective any more because everyone else is doing it. You should be ok with experimentation, exploration, and unorthodox tests. Remember: in the 1980s, it actually wasn't cool to be in software. It was dorky. That's why you could write basic scripts and amass a net worth of a hundred million bucks. Nowadays, everybody's doing it so the upside isn't the same.*

# UNORTHODOXY

# Section 2: The Internet

# Chapter 6: Most People Are Stupid...

One year, we had a company retreat in Sharm el-Sheikh. It was purely coincidental that we were there just before the twentieth anniversary of September 11th, an event that triggered two decades of violent changes that were, without an exception, bad news for just about everyone.

I call it a "company retreat" because the entirety of Discosloth (plus spouses) were there, we talked about industry-related things like Google Ads in between snorkeling and camel riding, and honestly what's better than a tax deductible week on the Red Sea?

Sharm el-Sheikh is a dusty and hot place on the southern tip of the Sinai Peninsula in Egypt, known for being the place where international summits happen in one of the many hotels or convention centers scattered down the coast.

Security is tight there, as you'd expect from a place sandwiched in between Israel, Egypt, Saudi Arabia, and Jordan. The authorities have even erected a patrolled border around the town — to prevent Bedouins from blowing things up.

As is common in most places other than the secure west, cars and shuttles go through security before being allowed onto hotel property. As we were heading back to the airport, I noticed that the hotel guard was using an ADE 651 bomb detector on the vehicle.

Just to disperse your doubts, I don't usually know the names of bomb detection devices. But this one has a story behind it.

The ADE 651 is a metal rod attached to a plastic handgrip. No batteries, no electronics, nothing. It is literally only a flimsy extendable metal stick glued onto the same type of grip that screws on top of a bottle of Windex. Yet the manufacturer (Advanced Tactical Security & Communications Ltd) claims that it can detect explosives, bodies, drugs, currency, or animals from distances up to three miles away.

The ADE 651 is nothing more than a dowsing rod: the sticks witches use to find locations to drill water wells.

These bomb detectors were created by a former British cop named James McCormick who sold these devices for as much as $60,000 each throughout the Middle East. The Iraqi government spent over $52,000,000 of *your* tax dollars on these devices (think about how many bags of rice that could have bought). And get this: the government of Jordan legally requires hotels to check cars with an ADE 651 before allowing parking in underground lots.

Anyone with half a brain can tell these things are a complete scam — right?

Before you think that only a bunch of rag-tag Middle Eastern governments were duped by the ADE 651, police departments in

Belgium used it to detect drugs...the Hong Kong government uses them...and even the US Army was almost convinced, until they spent several million (of *your* tax dollars) running actual tests to prove its inefficiency.[11]

James McCormick is currently languishing in prison for fraud.

If you dig into the details of how ATSC Ltd says these things work, it continues to blow your mind with the pure stupidity of the thing. In order to "program" the device to recognize other materials, you put samples of the desired material in a jar alongside a little paper sticker, shake it up, and let it sit for a few days, then stick the sticker on the device. I'm pretty sure a moderately intelligent toddler could see through this.

The interesting thing to me isn't that someone scammed a bunch of equipment purchasing departments. That seems like a pretty easy path to wealth. It's not that governments were duped. That, also, seems pretty easy.

The interesting thing to me is that this security guard really believes that this thing works, and he is using this piece of plastic with a metal stick every single day of his life. This is a man who goes home to a wife and kids every night. This is a man who knows how to fasten his belt and tie his shoes. This is a man who drives a stick shift. How does this security guard, by all accounts a normal functioning human with a normal job, ever get fooled by this plastic stick-on-a-grip? Does he know it's just theater? Does he just go with

---

[11] *"The story of the fake bomb detectors", BBC News, October 3rd, 2014.*

the flow for the paycheck? Or has he truly been bamboozled?

I have more confidence in a minimum-wage hotel security guard's analytical skills than the entire Iraqi government. Yet this fellow, his manager, and the management of the hotel collectively decided they would rather arm their guard with an expensive dummy device than with something like…you know…a German Shepard?

So what's the moral to this story?

Whenever you feel safe, protected, warm, and happy, you should know that smart people are protecting you. The pre-eminent experts of entire countries have entrusted your safety to a glorified dowsing rod.

Nothing is to be feared.

Just hush and move along.

Back to bell curves: we assume that intelligence, among other things, is evenly distributed across a gentle, symmetrical curve.

Even disregarding the fact that it's very hard to measure intelligence (and even more difficult to measure street smarts or wisdom) my theory is that due to hard cut-offs on the lower ends of all spectrums, the curse of mediocrity is worse than statistics would have you think.

Here's how this affects the internet, which, as I've mentioned, is dying.[12]

I have been on the internet since approximately 2003. I took

---

[12] *Of course it's not actually dying. Let me indulge in hyperbole.*

advantage of this internet access from an early age, back when a teenager could build a simple HTML website and charge a small business thousands for it.

I have seen channels and platforms and mediums come and go. But over time, the ups and downs are smoothed out, and you can easily see a certain trajectory. In the case of the internet, over the past two decades, there is one clear trajectory: it is going from decentralization to centralization.

The internet used to be composed of independent forums and blogs, which largely created permanent content that was accessible by the entire world. It is now composed of approximately a dozen centralized platforms, where most people engage in comments and produce ephemeral content that is only accessible after login by people with user accounts on that particular platform, and disappears in the bowels of the platform after a week or two.

The barrier to entry used to be massive. It would cost tens of thousands of dollars to develop an e-commerce website. Now, you simply need $30 for a Shopify account with performance and optimization that is unrivaled by any other possibility.

Most people are stupid.

And now they're on the internet.

## Chapter 6 Summary

*The internet is changing. Adoption rates are skyrocketing, which brings a certain "tyranny of the masses". Barriers to entry are low, in both a technological and financial sense. This means that much more effort (or capital) is required in order to separate yourself from the teeming masses of netizens who also want to start a marketing agency, sell shoes, write articles, upload videos, or whatever else people are doing on the internet these days.*

# Chapter 7: ...And Now They're On The Internet

I've often mentioned how I miss the *old* internet.

And the "old internet" that I remember wasn't even the *truly* old internet. It was just the internet pre-Facebook, pre-Twitter, and pre-social media in general.

The internet's greatest feature (that it's a network anyone can access) is ultimately becoming one of its greatest hindrances (now that everyone has accessed it).

Before September of 1993, internet access was almost exclusively relegated to academia: mostly, users at universities communicating via Usenet (a distributed discussion system first launched in 1980).

Throughout the 1980s, every September, incoming freshmen at MIT or Stanford would get internet access for the first time in their lives, and a noticeable few weeks of Usenet chaos would erupt as these new users struggled to learn netiquette. Eventually, people would either learn to behave themselves properly, or get tired of Usenet and leave.

This left a small, monolithic, and homogenous user base.

Accordingly, Usenet was generally helpful, informative, self-moderating, and intelligent.

Until September 1993.

AOL opened up internet access to new users that September. Anyone who was around in the early 90s remembers the countless floppy disks and CD-ROMs that you'd get in the mail.

AOL spent over $300 million sending out those disks. At one point, AOL was responsible for purchasing over 50% of the entire world's manufacturing supply of CD-ROMs, and onboarded a new internet user every six seconds.

Someone coined the term "Eternal September" since it was now an endless start-of-semester chaos. Millions of internet freshmen, from all ages and walks of life, were swamping the old habits, etiquette and behavioral expectations.

The phrase Eternal September has now evolved to describe what happens when a large user base adopts a new platform. Generally, it's a deluge that destroys the existing culture. It's sort of like what happens when a new condo is constructed in a sleepy beachfront town...a lot of people in Yukon XLs drive down from Oklahoma every summer and start demanding bigger margaritas.

For most of us, an influx of users that large is a problem we'd love to have (if you own a small coffee shop and you suddenly get hundreds of folks lined up out the door, you forget about culture and you start making drinks).

It gets tricky when we aren't being rewarded for the influx (in other words, if we're just part of a community rather than profiting directly from it).

It's hard to complain about hundreds of folks lined up out the door when you own the coffee shop, but if you're a daily regular, your relaxing mornings formerly spent working on your laptop in the corner turns into misery. Suddenly, you aren't the regular anymore.

A few years ago, one of my friends started a blog-turned-Facebook-group. Originally slanted more towards satire and oddball gossip than anything else, it was a quirky local forum for the in-crowd. Over the course of a few years, it grew into a local news monstrosity with over 50,000 members, providing the sort of info on local corruption, unsolved crimes, scandals, and general depraved behavior that is missing from your standard syndicated news sources.

As these tens of thousands of members accumulated, the group's exclusivity and character were diluted.

The concept of satire was lost. If my friend posted a ridiculous story faithful to the original roots of the group (say, diatribes about the Toilet Thieves of Hangar Hill, or conjecture about what sorts of unpleasant things are hidden in the crawlspaces of the rich and famous) it was guaranteed to ruffle the feathers of at least a dozen suburban moms, and probably a city council member or two.

It's almost impossible to retain your vibe — avoiding your *own* Eternal September, in a way — if you don't control the platform.

Whether that's billions of people on the internet, or 50,000 residents on a local forum, sometimes too much is too much.

How does that apply to those of us with online agendas? It doesn't matter what your agenda is. Maybe you're running a small ecommerce business. Maybe you're trying to make an altruistic difference in the world. Maybe you're running Google Ads. Maybe you're trying to recruit members into your end-times cult. Whatever it is, it's getting harder and harder to do something successful on the internet.

You pretty much can't do it without a full-blown marketing campaign, a fat budget, press coverage, and corporate sponsorship.

Going viral used to mean you'd have years of internet fame. But that's because there was nothing else to go viral.

Now, there are 900,000 things going viral, for about two minutes each. And you'll forget about every one of them three minutes from now.

My conclusion of the state of the internet is that it's too late to save it, at least in its original state. The internet has to start over.

There needs to be Usenet 2.0, on an entirely different technology stack. The internet has to reinvent itself, or it will crumble. And then again, maybe in 20 or 30 years, re-invent itself again. And again.

The internet is at a curious place, that's to be sure.

The slow change from decentralization to centralization, from independent nodes to platform-centric content, changes the way digital marketers *market.*

During the heyday of digital marketing, smart marketers could make tens of millions simply by doing something nobody else had done. Everything was low-hanging fruit. You could simply think "I'm going to sell Norwegian children's clothing online in the United States" and because the idea was decent, and nobody else was doing it, you'd sell a million dollars a year of little woolen baby sweaters.

Now, there are approximately a thousand other people trying to do the same thing, so you'll be lucky to sell anything at all unless you outperform, out-strategize, out-advertise, and out-deliver across all fronts. As I tell ecommerce operators on a regular basis, it used to take twenty thousand bucks and a couple years to build up a great ecommerce website, but now all it takes is $30 and a Shopify subscription.

The former focus on growth marketing is tightening. I'm not saying it's gone, but it's simply far more competitive.

The only solution? You have to pursue un-scalable, highly difficult paths. You have to find an "edge" that is *not* easy. Your differentiator needs to be something only you can do. You have to make sure you're not clumped at the bottom of that conceptual curve.

What does this look like in practice? Here's a few ideas.

One of the ways to differentiate is *niche*. This has been the classic way of differentiating oneself, as first made popular in the 2006 book

*The Long Tail* by *Wired* editor-in-chief Chris Anderson.[13]

The long-tail concept was revolutionary in 2006, which believe it or not, was nearly two decades ago. It no longer applies on the internet as we know it today. In 2005, only 51% of the developed world was on the Internet. In 2023, 93% of the developed world is on the Internet.[14]

That's a massive increase. But here's the kicker. In 2005, only 2% of Africa and 9% of Asia had access to the internet. In 2023, this number has increased to 37% and 67%, respectively. All in all, over 5 billion internet users were added in this period.

Access to the internet has clearly been beneficial to the world, and enabled literally billions of people to learn, build, work, and connect. But it's also commoditized the internet. Access to *(and even familiarity of)* the internet used to be a huge barrier to entry. Now there is none.

That doesn't mean there isn't a possibility of finding a niche anymore. It just means you will likely need to focus on a niche that is already highly selective and rare, leveraging your unique knowledge and passion of very specific skillsets or pursuits.

Another way to differentiate is *skill*. We've touched on this idea by referencing the idea of universal bell curves being deceptive at best. Although billions of people have entered the digital domain and

---

[13] *The Long Tail: Why the Future of Business Is Selling Less of More. Chris Anderson, 2006.*

[14] *"Measuring digital development: Facts and figures". Telecommunication Development Bureau, 2023.*

are technically competing with you, the reality is that most are clumped on the far lower side of the curve. For better or worse, *most* people are still hard up against that hard bottom cut-off. Just because someone has access to a mobile device and can swipe on TikTok, for example, does not mean that they are particularly skilled at using the full potential of the internet.[15]

Pursuing domain knowledge is still massively effective. Simply by expending the energy required to develop your skills, your knowledge, and gain real-world experience still launches someone into the far upper end of the "bell curve".

And another way, of course, is *brand*. This is very difficult for a number of reasons, and I believe that it is the only marketing and sales asset that can be translated universally across platforms, channels, skillsets, and niches.

Here is why brand is difficult: many people are bad at developing their brand, many people hate communication, many people are not self-aware, and many people resist the idea of having to *sell* their own expertise. I don't blame them, but the reality is that having your own circle of people who listen to you, talk with you, teach you, learn from you, buy from you, and sell to you creates a sort of personal economy in which you can make things happen simply by communication.

Branding often gets a bad rap. It's seen as vague. But that's only because people have seen so much bad branding. Real branding is

---

[15] *Or their brain.*

simply storytelling.

And you want to make sure to tell your own story, otherwise others will tell that story for you.

---

## Chapter 7 Summary

*The internet now is platform-based, rather than decentralized. The only way to succeed on a crowded internet is by simply being better: whether that's finding a very specific niche, improving your skills tremendously, or building a brand that survives across platforms and channels. What does this mean practically? Platforms change, platforms die. If you want your brand to outlast the platforms, you must find a way to transcend them. Don't put all your eggs into one basket.*

# Chapter 8: The Lying Internet Theory

The internet of yesterday wasn't bulletproof, but you might say it was bullet-resistant.

The internet of today is increasingly fragile.

Even if your bread & butter isn't *The Internet*, this matters more than you might think. Whether you're a marketer, or a small business owner, or even just some dude furiously typing out frantic tweets and hitting "send" to a small but rapidly growing follower count, the internet is where stuff happens.[16] And your control of it is slipping away, whether you know it or not.

The internet of yesterday was stronger for a few reasons.

This is not because it was highly regulated (it wasn't) or because it was particularly well engineered (it wasn't) or because it ran on a dependable, reliable infrastructure (it didn't).

The reason the original internet was so strong (the internet before the late 90s, at least) was because it was actually as close to a decentralized, distributed model of computing as we've ever seen. It

---

[16] *I'm @gilgildner*

didn't rely upon monolithic entities to host, index, search, and serve information to the end user.

The original internet was just a bunch of people with modems, dialing into servers (which were really just loud, beige Pentium I computers running in someone's basement).

As the internet has matured, it's taken a lot of steps towards security and reliability and redundancy — but it's actually becoming considerably less bulletproof.

It's regulated now (and as we saw in various Arab Spring uprisings, or as we see with China's Great Firewall, or India, or Iran, or Venezuela, or Uganda) many governments shut down internet access entirely. At the very least, every government's security apparatus is heavily monitoring just what citizens are interested in.

It's also monolithic now, both in organizational and practical forms. For example, the most perennially concerning is ICANN, the Internet Corporation for Assigned Names and Numbers. Since 1998, ICANN has enjoyed a dubious pseudo-governmental power to control the domains and routing of the internet. Who wants an un-elected, un-governable, and un-fireable body that's in charge of our domain names?

Another chokepoint is the proliferation of CDNs (content distribution networks) which cache websites for more efficient distribution, or even security applications that are almost universally installed. It's a technological advantage to serve websites across a global cache, to be sure, but that's like owning a bakery and then hiring a middleman to stand between your customer and the counter, handing out donuts as they see fit. Maybe it's efficient, but it's another step. What happens if your donut man just decides to walk away? Cloudflare has the most internet endpoints of any entity in the world. What happens when they go down?[17]

Hosts have been reduced to a few colossal services like AWS (33% market share) or Microsoft Azure (18%) or Google Cloud (10%) or IBM (6%) or Alibaba (5%).

On the consumption side of the internet, another chokepoint is the reduction of ISPs. Whereas you used to have access through your local ISP (pretty much whoever gave you phone service) these have been slowly consolidated into a handful of titans. The chances that your internet access is controlled by Time Warner, Verizon, or Comcast is insanely high.

Online content used to be published on sites written and hosted by the authors themselves: remember the old internet where every website looked different and you surfed the net through many different domains all day? Now, this content is ephemeral and mostly on Facebook, Instagram, or Twitter.

All of that to say…your options are narrowing. The variety is gone.

The netizen of 1996 likely ran their site on their own server, on a local ISP, on a private platform, on their own machine, and processed

---

[17] *In 2024, a bug stemming from security firm CrowdStrike slapped the blue screen of death on millions of Microsoft PCs worldwide (but only if they were connected to the internet).*

transactions through their bank's merchant card provider. The mailman brought letters in a respectable-looking and very square truck.

The netizen of today just uploads stuff to Facebook, Snapchat, or TikTok, and hopes Stripe processes everything correctly.

The internet started as a decentralized system. It's now anything but that.

It may be easier, and more streamlined, now.

But it's also fragile.

Twenty or thirty years ago, the internet exploded, and everyone who could click "publish" suddenly had a global audience. The democratization of communication isn't new. It's super dangerous, after all, to give the common people the freedom to communicate. Institutions, which are built on archaic systems, start to fail.

That's why there is so much resistance to new forms of communication.

Just like Gutenberg's press brought down the supremacy of the Roman Catholic Church, a hulking institution that had been built on centuries of information control, email and internet has now done the same for a few different sorts of modern-day institutions.

When people circumvent the mainstream method of information consumption (up until the late 1990s that was radio, television, and newspapers) then the status quo begins to fall apart.

It's not some malicious conspiracy. It's just the way of the world.

Institutions control the zeitgeist: the money comes from somewhere. It's no secret why high-flying PR firms charge millions a year to develop a narrative for their high-flying clients.

When new technology comes along, however, there's always an adoption delay. The 16-year-old acne-pocked hacker kid finds out about the internet long before the old fart running a PR consultancy in Washington. This delay in adoption means that entire news channels are suddenly created from popular social media profiles. Billion dollar brands are created from email newsletters. Blogs become authoritative entities. People start making more money (and have more journalistic freedom) posting on X or Substack than they did working at *The New York Times*.[18]

Right now, people are upset about people posting whatever they want online. No accountability. No fact-checking. No proof. It's the Wild West out there. But we don't police the right of your average crazy man on the sidewalk from being incorrect: why should we police any other medium of communication?

I would like to fight for the right to be wrong. I'd like people to be able to have wrong opinions, and even be able to express them.

Secret opinions are incredibly toxic. Held within, secret opinions are like information ulcers that boil up and make actual bad things happen. If one of my acquaintances thinks something crazy...like "dogs are vessels of alien souls and must be exterminated" then I

---

[18] *If you ever see outrage, before you hop on the anger bandwagon, look for motive.*

would prefer he be able to express those opinions freely. Before he comes over to my house and attacks our dog. My wife would be so upset. I wouldn't hear the end of it.

That's why I keep a few *wrong* folks in my social feeds.

As a form of balance. Information yin/yang, you might say.

There's a couple fellows who are so absolutely wrong on everything they say, that I keep them visible so that I can be reminded how ignorance is intrinsic to humanity. These are the sorts of fellows who are overeducated, underemployed, and overconfident.

Yet I would like them to stay free. No fact checking. Just spewing their views into the universe.

Adding a gatekeeper to information (press, media, academia, tech companies) does not solve the problem. Inserting an arbiter of truth into the flow of information (by checking facts) does not solve the core issue. The problem is not fake news, propaganda, outright lies, or ignorant viral posts.

The problem are gullible people who don't know how to analyze things critically, and who aren't skeptical enough.

Fact checking is just trying to intercept lies before they get to people. It's a stop-gap measure. It will inevitably fail. Instead of addressing people's responses to those lies, fact checking (or gatekeeping information, by anointing yourself the accredited press) is like popping aspirin for a headache when you have a railroad spike embedded in your medulla oblongata.

Lies have been there from the beginning. We're not going to stop the lies.

We can only try to prevent ourselves from falling for them.

This fragile internet is full of lies. It's also full of facts. And that's something probably worth touching on in the next chapter: how people lie with true data.

---

## Chapter 8 Summary

*There is a certain level of innate trust that the early internet fostered. This came from a shared ethos. You assumed the person on the other side of the screen was at least a semi-functional human. I no longer believe this trust exists. This has changed how we market, sell, and brand ourselves online. On the new, dying internet you must come across not just as a likable person, but as a real person.*

# Chapter 9: Lying With Data

Bell curves are the easy way out.

You've seen bell curves attempt to visualize distributions in almost every discipline: a gentle swell in the middle of the graph, right at the 50th percentile, portrays the concept that "most people are in the middle".

While this does happen from time to time, I actually think we've become conditioned to think of *everything* as bell curves.

Let me illustrate.

If you were to judge people on their ability to shoot a gun accurately at a target, the default idea is that most people will be "just okay" at it, perhaps neither great or terrible, but just in the middle. You can probably visualize a bell curve.

I have taken many, many new shooters to the range.[19] And I can attest (I believe most other shooters would agree) that actually people are either very bad or very good. If you were to graph it, I think there would be a massive lump of terrible shooters at the bottom quintile,

---

[19] *America.*

and a small but noticeable spike of fantastic shooters at the top quintile.

I don't know if I've ever seen a new shooter be *average* at shooting a gun. They are either dangerously inept (the sort of person who picks up a gun, racks the slide, and savagely shoots the ground) or someone who can reliably hit the bullseye within a magazine's worth of practice.

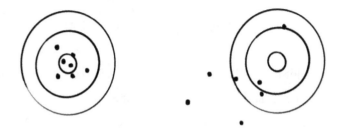

*It's either/or. I don't know if I've ever seen a new shooter anywhere in between these two extremes.*

It doesn't matter how intelligent you are: if you can't apply that intelligence to the real world in a pragmatic, analytical, and collaborative manner, that intelligence is worth absolutely nothing.

Perhaps you are the world's foremost expert in creating marketing dashboards in some business intelligence software, your IQ has been measured into the stratosphere, you earned degrees from the most distinguished universities, and perhaps you've written papers on the most cutting-edge strategies in your industry. It doesn't matter a bit. You won't gain anything from that repository of accumulated knowledge, unless you also have the critical thinking to apply it to real-life problems, in ways that help you (or others) build things.

Data itself isn't the goal: the goal is deploying that data into real-world scenarios.

Data itself can be cherry-picked, which turns technical truths into practical lies.

Data means little without interpretation: and interpretation requires wisdom. And wisdom? Well, countless tomes of literature have been written on the topic since antiquity, so I won't make any significant headway on it, but it's safe to say that the acquisition of wisdom is a lot harder than the acquisition of knowledge. Sometimes it just comes the hard way, through trial and error, experience and observation, failure and success.

Critical thinking is so important in the digital economy, especially since it's so easy to default to relying on metrics to prove success. But rarely do we look at those metrics ("time on page" or "return on ad spend" or "engagement rate" or "impression share") and then critically examine whether we need to be measuring them at all, and if so, *why?*

Critical thinking is just taking gritty details, and going backwards until we see the big picture. Critical thinking helps you get out of the weeds. Critical thinking helps you realize what your goal should actually be, and then helps you get there.

I want to look at how sometimes people lie to you via telling the truth (by cherry-picking data); how sometimes experts aren't really who you think they are (trust should be based on the veracity of what they've said, rather than credentials alone), and how it's usually better to look at the holistic big picture rather than the small details.

As I've mentioned before, data itself is worthless.

I'll have to admit that I do really love data. The older I get, the more I realize that good data can help inform most decisions.

But without a proper, unbiased, bird's-eye-view analysis, reinforced by real-world experience, this data is absolutely worthless. It's actually worse than worthless. If I'm faced with a decision, I'd rather someone tell me an outright lie rather than give me technically true data flavored by a biased analysis.

Analysis affects everything.

If a marketing agency cherry picks the data to report to a client, it affects the client's understanding of their ROI.

If a news company publishes reports with drastic numbers, it is often pure clickbait meant to monger fear.

We are faced with an onslaught of data every day, and yet it doesn't really inform our decision making (or ultimately make our lives any better) unless we know how to correctly interpret the information we're given.

Every news article you read contains conclusions derived from data. Every performance report you get from a vendor contains results derived from data. Every think tank publishes policy pieces derived from data.

Rarely does anyone outright *lie*. They just cherry pick their data points.

Nobody falsifies data…they just *creatively interpret* data.

That's why the presentation and analysis of data—combined with anecdotal, boots-on-the-ground experience—can be more important than the actual data itself.

The other day a friend sent me an article by a German psychologist that shows how "instinct", or gut feelings driven by experience, can actually be more effective over time than making business decisions driven solely by algorithms or formulas.

Embracing your experience (gut instinct and anecdotal experience) helps you flag questionable statistics.

Earlier I mentioned how when I'm faced with making an important decision, and I'm trying to gather evidence, I would much rather be blatantly lied to than presented with true cherry-picked facts.

Take digital marketing as an example. A new client sent me the past year of analytics reports for their website, as delivered by their previous agency.

I noticed that instead of reporting the metrics from January 1st through December 31st, as is the honest way to report results, the agency reported January 1st through January 31st of the next year. They presented *January to January* performance which sounds logical, but in reality a true 365-day report would be *January through December* performance.

It seems minor. Perhaps an oversight. But that extra thirty-one days, which most people won't notice, improved that agency's annual sales numbers to a total of 10,098 conversions. If you re-calculated the performance from January 1st through December 31st, you got a number of 9,811 conversions.

The simple, silly reality is that 10,098 looks a whole lot bigger than 9,811. Those extra thirty-one days were just enough to improve the "annual" metrics by ~8% and tip a few of those metrics over the 10,000 mark.

It's really that silly.

It's a lie, via a nugget of truth, and all the previous agency does with this lie was kick their contract can down the road. Eventually the client's experiential wisdom kicks in ("wait a second, we're actually not making *that* much money!") and eventually they fire the old agency and send Discosloth an email.

Sometimes you'll see news stories reporting a 75% increase in homicides this year. Yet, if you look at a wider perspective, and zoom out to a 20 year pattern, you might see that it's just an aberrant spike this year (a drug deal gone bad, or a crazy man on bath salts) and homicides are actually falling across the board.

You'll see news stories reporting that new tax laws will only affect those who make over $400,000 per year...and technically, that's true, if you're talking *only* about federal income tax, or capping of tax credits even for lower income folks. No mention is made of increasing capital gains tax, which trickles down and affects everyone…or of the fact that inflationary currency devaluation continually reduces what $400,000 really means.

We must be highly critical of any data thrown our way.

But what if we can't all become statisticians? What if we don't have time to analyze the raw data? (I don't!)

There are some code words to look out for. Clues that will alert you to the possibility of a viewpoint being inserted into the results.

First are qualifiers. These are words like "up to", "nearly", "around", "almost", or "between".

Second are emotional words. These are words like "massive", "underwhelming", "shocking", or "minuscule".

Third are super-specifics. If you read an article that says 44 people murdered in one day in Chicago, it makes Chicago seem very dangerous. It's a clickbait title. Perhaps 44 people were murdered on a very bad day, but it doesn't mean it's the *usual*.

Fourth are averages. If someone says the average American makes $41,000 per year, that's quite meaningless. Who is an "average" American? The better question is what is the median wage — and further, make sure that is counting all the requisite parameters. Is that counting part-time employment, high schoolers, pensions, Social Security? Do they live in Nebraska or New York City? Remember the duplicity of bell curve thinking. Many folks don't make any money at all, and many folks make millions.[20]

---

[20] *If you look at an income distribution graph from the U.S. Census Bureau, as a matter of fact it's not a bell curve at all. It's heavy at the very bottom, with a long, stretched out upper end with a few very large spikes in the far billions.*

Here are two facts:

— *87,647 people die from diabetes every year in the US.*
— *Over 800,000 Americans per year die with diabetes.*

Both of these statements are true. The difference is simply in the goalposts. How do you categorize a death?[21] It's clear that diabetes is a problem. But how you define that problem (and how you interpret it) tells two different stories.

Only 10-15% of people with diabetes will die *specifically* from diabetes. In the other 85-90%, the actual cause of death will be from co-morbidities: cardiac, obesity, pulmonary, digestive issues.

It's a tricky question, because you can keep going backwards. Did someone die from arterial clogging, or did their arteries start getting clogged because they had diabetes? Did they get diabetes because they didn't control their sugar intake in early life? Ultimately, do we blame the daily Pepsi and donut that they consumed every day in the 1960s?

So how many people die *from* diabetes? That has to do with whether you're asking a doctor with the American Diabetes Association, or the American Heart Association.

Neither will lie to you.

But both will be biased.

---

[21] *"Diabetes Report Card." Centers for Disease Control and Prevention, 2022*

There are hard lower limits to almost any form of measurement. But there are not necessarily hard upper limits.

Take health, for example. If you were to try to visualize people's state of health, you could plot them linearly. But here's the thing: there is a hard cutoff on the bottom end, but there really isn't a hard cutoff on the top end. The bottom end is death. You can't get any unhealthier. The bottom end of the health curve goes fairly rapidly from immobility, to catatonic state, to being very, very dead. But you can always get a bit healthier and stronger and energetic. There isn't an absolute top.

So how do we realistically graph this sort of distribution across a curve? If at all, it means that there should be a huge lump on the bottom half of the curve, with a very long upper tail of people who are progressively healthier and stronger. It probably looks a lot more like a tadpole than a symmetrical curve.

This is also applicable to intelligence (it's easy to find many instances of the absolutely brain-dead, but it's not as easy to find the smartest or the most mathematical) and it's applicable to money (at the bottom cutoff, it is easy to have no money, but it is difficult to ever get the *mostest*).

And it's applicable to marketing and sales.

Marketers and brand owners often take the easy way out by (directly or indirectly) comparing performance to benchmarks and baselines. But this is a cop-out.

The only benchmark that really matters will always concern *your* specific goals. As long as *you* are profitable, as long as *your* business is happy, as long as *you* can scale at the speed you want to scale, why do we focus so strongly on benchmarks? Why do we use arbitrary KPIs as stand-ins?

It's not that key performance indicators or industry benchmarks aren't useful. They can be very useful in the right hands. It's that they're so often used as crutches to mask actual health.

Don't let the bean counters ruin your company.

---

## Chapter 9 Summary

*One of the reasons that digital marketing began to quickly eclipse traditional marketing was attribution: the ability to track conversions and performance so accurately across multiple channels, platforms, and mediums. For the first few years, this was a huge selling point. But as it turns out, it may have been a short-term win for digital marketers, at the cost of long-term success. In recent years, it's become difficult to attribute with the accuracy we were used to. This is because the internet is now centralized rather than decentralized. When you work within the constraints of platforms like Google, Facebook, Instagram, Shopify, TikTok, or any other centralized companies, of course they're going to limit the access to data. We've given up granular data in the name of convenience. And this segregation and obscuration of data makes it very easy to be misled by numbers. The forest for the trees, so to speak.*

## Chapter 10: The Death of the Persona

The world's power structure is (and always has been) pure feudalism.

Most reasonable readers will have an instinctive knee-jerk reaction to that statement. It grates against our very democratic bones. But as the famous line in *The Princess Bride* goes, "life *is* pain, Your Highness, and anybody who tells you different is selling something."

We can mask it with pleasantries all we want, but at the end of the day we're all still serfs, merchants, and nobles. Unless you are a very special person (in which case you wouldn't be reading this book, and instead be breakfasting with parliament members) you are probably an average merchant just like me. The only difference is now we have drive-through coffee kiosks and phones pre-installed with TikTok.

*So*, you ask? Get your strange political statements out of here! But there's a method to the madness, and it ultimately comes down to the lens through which you view the world generally, and human behavior specifically.

I have discovered that viewing human behavior with an assumption of uninhibited free will and total agency produces unrealistic expectations of results. Approaching every human interaction by assuming that every person is a free agent is a major assumption.

Now, to be clear, I don't actually know for sure if we do have total free will and philosophical agency.[22] All I know is that pragmatically, out here in the streets, it sure doesn't feel like it. We're dependent upon many other external factors (expectations, economies, social pressures, jealousies, demands). So it's useful to build a framework (even if it's just an experiment) to see if this lens changes any expectations.

Say you're an advertiser, advertising widgets. You want your ads to result in purchases. What happens if you assume every human is different, that everyone has the choice to buy or not, that everyone has a special perspective, that every human is a unique snowflake? The answer: marketers attempt to create unique personas for each customer.

For well on two decades, the idea of the Ideal Customer Persona has been a central pillar of marketing. For years, marketers have created dozens of these special personas with catchy handles like Stay-At-Home Sharon or Student Sally or Professional Pete. They then attempt to assign intents, desires, resources, and customer journeys to each of these personas, and try to market to each of them

---

[22] *Or even care.*

individually.

One of my most controversial marketing opinions is that customer personas are a crock of crap. First, the quantification of people isn't that easy, and second, it assumes that people actually are that different.[23]

But what if it were far simpler? What if people just buy stuff because they want it? What if they buy stuff because they need it? What if they adjust *their* expectations to *your* brand, rather than you adjusting *your* brand to *their* expectations?

Humans are scattered so disparately across the behavioral curve that it's a huge waste of energy to try to reach every single one of them exactly where they are.

Much of the stuff that seems to define humanity is merely a facade. People are people. Just like we're all serfs, and democracy is merely an illusion of choice layered on top, I really think that most brands would be better suited just being more of their own brand, and attracting those who happen to like their vibe.

We take advantage of user segmentation in many of our campaigns. It works better in some than others.

For example, we run recruitment campaigns for one of the world's fastest growing hedge funds, hiring highly quantitative researchers in a highly technical niche. Finding and hiring these

---

[23] *Most people aren't different. They're clumped with lots of others. Understanding how most folks are clumped across the bell curve will go a long way for marketers.*

technical quants is very tricky, and as it turns out, *very* expensive. In this scenario, user segmentation makes sense, because there are only so many quants in the world.

But we also run the advertising campaigns for a large beauty brand, with almost a hundred physical locations and an ecommerce storefront. Segmentation oddly enough makes far less sense here, even if you'd think it would. After all, only men use beard balm, right? Wrong. As it turns out, sometimes grandmothers buy it for their grandsons, girlfriends buy it for their boyfriends, and mothers buy it for their sons. After all, it's not like persona targeting is really so granular and accurate that we can select "has a big beard" from within our campaign targeting settings.

What is oddly far more important for a company like this is *branding*, which brings me to an entire chapter on why awareness-based marketing and advertising is somehow *still* criminally underrated.

---

**Chapter 10 Summary**

*People are not that different. The development of the ICP (Ideal Customer Persona) was a clever thought which probably was the single-handed most destructive trend for digital marketers in the past decade. As it turns out, building a dozen marketing and sales strategies around targeting one specific sort of person is ironically less effective than simply coming up with a single marketing strategy for your whole brand. Would you rather fish through a bucket of construction debris with your fingers looking for a screw, or drag a magnet that attracts all the screws?*

# Chapter 11: Building Brands

If you have made it through the past few chapters, you've likely come away with a sense of impending doom, or you think I'm a sociopath who clearly doesn't hold humanity in very high regard, especially after that "people are stupid" chapter.

But I actually really love humans. I am just painfully self-aware. I don't want to delude myself (or anyone else) that we're particularly unique or special. Only with a clear-sighted knowledge of our limitations can you really make the correct decisions about whatever you're involved with (sales, marketing, investing, how much ribeye you should buy for this weekend, or if it's really worth going into debt for that bigger house).

Perhaps the most sociopathic thing that I will say in this book is this: *most humans actually aren't very interesting.*

This is good for you and I, who want nothing more than to market and to sell.

It means that the threshold for interestingness is very low. You do not have to do much in order to become interesting. You just have to be a bit different.

You may not even realize how uninteresting most people are because, by definition, you're only noticing the interesting ones. In the course of an average day, I probably see hundreds of faces: a few while walking the dog, a few at the coffee shop, a few at Whole Foods, a few folks when I meet up with friends for a drink, and all the ones in between. I don't remember *most* of those people, however. That's not because I don't like them. It's because nothing about them signaled the importance of remembering their face.

So who *do* you remember? You remember those who went out of their way to talk to you. You remember those who wore clothes or behaved noticeably different than most others. You remember those who are either uncommonly beautiful or uncommonly ugly. You remember those who are anachronistic. You remember those who bother you, or those who intrigue you.

Now, the catch is that you should never *try* to be different. Trying to be different is what teenagers do, and it's cringe-inducing precisely because they're trying so hard. I'm sure you've met a grown man who's trying a bit too hard to fit into an image: perhaps he thinks of himself as an intellectual, so he wears a cardigan, thick-rimmed glasses, and twirls his moustache while bringing up obscure facts about Heidegger. Or perhaps he thinks of himself as some sort of alpha operator, so he wears olive drab and boots and wears a fixed-blade knife strapped to his military belt. Or perhaps he thinks of himself as the second coming of Seth Godin, and he shaves his head, rolls up his sleeves, dons a pair of thick-rimmed spectacles, and does lots of yoga hand gestures.

Differentness bubbles up from within, and this applies to brands and companies just as much as it applies to people.

I'm a firm believer that neither you (nor a branding firm) can *actually* create an authentic brand from scratch. You actually have to *be* what you portray, and then make sure people know about who you really are. Otherwise, you are really no more truly special than a bag of potato crisps with a new design.

Your brand is the story other people tell about you.

In 1910, one in every 11 Americans was either born in Germany, or their parents were German. There were American cities called Berlin, American rivers named the Rhine, hundreds of Germantowns, and millions of Americans named Schmidt, Mueller, Schwartz, and Zimmerman. German was the most common spoken language outside of English. Lutherans and Catholics owned thousands of biergartens and breweries across the US.

Ten years later, the Rhine was renamed the Marne, the Germantowns were renamed to Pershing or Garland, and suddenly a lot more Americans were called Smith, Miller, Black, and Carpenter.

Of course, what happened in the middle of those ten years has a lot to do with it, but it changed the course of American history afterwards.

The reputation of both Lutherans and Catholics plunged, the

temperance movement demonized both alcohol and more permissive European lifestyles (almost entirely spearheaded by middle-aged Protestant spinsters), and the United States passed some of the most intrusive laws imaginable.

It was illegal to speak German on the phone in South Dakota. Alcohol became illegal. The first immigration laws established quotas in 1921. Widespread curfew laws were established.[24]

A hundred years later, does this matter?

Not really, if we're just talking about a name. It doesn't really matter that Mount Kitchener's original name was Kaiserstuhl.

But renaming happens all the time. It's the most desperate, last-ditch step in rebranding.

Have you ever wondered why the British royals use the last name "Windsor"? Seems such a British name, doesn't it? That's because it's entirely made up to sound British.

Until 1917, when King George changed his last name, the royals used the last name Saxe-Coburg und Gotha. Of course, in a world war where everyone was battling the armies of their cousins, that complicated the messaging. Bad optics, you know? So Georgie stripped his German cousins of their royal titles and changed his own last name to Windsor, prompting Kaiser Wilhelm II to joke that he was now looking forward to seeing Shakespeare's *The Merry Wives of Saxe-Coburg-Gotha.*

---

[24] *The Library of Congress. "Chronology : The Germans in America (European Reading Room, Library of Congress)." 2014*

Still — what does that have to do with any of us little folks, the sorts of serfs and merchants who don't have armies to attack our cousins with?

Rebranding.

Like when the Lance Armstrong Foundation changed its name to Livestrong because of his doping scandal. Or when GMAC had so much bad press from being bailed out by the government, they changed their name to Ally. Or when Valeant got bad PR for raising drug prices, so they switched to Bausch.

The thing is — changing your name is a last-ditch effort. If you're at the point that you're changing your name to avoid the stigma, you've already done something so terribly wrong that you're basically declaring bankruptcy on your whole identity.

It's like if I do something so embarrassing, that I change my name to Bob and move to Sudan. At that point, I'm admitting that I've so totally jumped the shark that my reputation is irretrievable. I'm starting over.

How does this tie into the renaming of cities, streets, and rivers? It's pretty terrible when someone rebrands your entire culture for you. I am sure none of the simple immigrant beer brewers in South Dakota had it out for Americans. They'd just come over here to make lots of money and get cheap land, and now they couldn't even legally speak German to themselves over the phone.

I'm positive it wasn't the Germans who voted on that law.

The point is that it doesn't take much for your story to be told for you. Whether you're a company trying to fashion a brand ethos...or a German immigrant brewing beer...or a freelancer trying to get more work...or a first-generation Mexican immigrant...it's rare that anyone is truly in charge of their own story.

Someone else is always out there, telling it for you.

That's the whole point of branding. Taking back what's yours. And that is also why I am no longer calling it liberty cabbage, like they did in the 1920s, or freedom fries, like they did in the 2000s. I'm sticking with sauerkraut and French fries.

You should be in total control of your own brand.

---

**Chapter 11 Summary**

*Branding is the single pursuit which will weather the storms of a dying internet. When your brand is authentic, true, and attractive, it's the only thing that can be translated across changing mediums and platforms. If Facebook dies, move your brand to X. If X dies, move your brand to an email newsletter. Or better yet, build your brand across all channels. Someone, somewhere will always be telling stories about you and your brand (whether this brand is your personal brand, or your business brand) so you might as well take control and fill that void with your own version of it.*

# Section 3: Unorthodox Sales & Marketing

# UNORTHODOXY

# Chapter 12: Selling Things Through Stories

Selling something is the act of trading one thing for another, like taking a piece of silver in exchange for a loaf of bread.

Marketing is the act of letting people know that the loaf of bread is for sale.

You can boil marketing down to four simple words: selling things through stories.[25]

The marketing is the first step in the sales process. You tell people about this loaf of bread, and hope they buy it. Perhaps they ask some questions about it, and then you answer.

The sale is the last step in the marketing process. You've told the story about the bread, and the sale is accepting the piece of silver.

The story, the tale through which you sell things, can take many forms. It can be descriptive (this bread is healthy, this bread is made from rye grain, this bread was baked this morning). It can be emotional (my wife baked this bread, it smells fantastic, it is made

---

[25] *One of my favorite ever reviews of a previous book was an anonymous one-star reviewer absolutely furious over this line. He said our definition "disregards an entire academic and professional Marketing community" but he couldn't even capitalize his words correctly.*

locally, it is her grandmother's recipe).

It can even be a blend of both, which is brand. And brand, when you boil it down, is just a certain pre-familiarity with the descriptions and emotions. At some point, when you've described the bread to enough people, and enough people have experienced the bread, it becomes *Annika's Bread*, and everybody already knows they're going to love it.

The questions you're answering start with *what is this bread*, then go towards *why should I buy this bread*, until finally you can answer *who made this bread?*

This is what marketing is: talking about stuff until you get money.

The further we stray from this truth, the further we stray from the light. We must be careful to not make this any more complex than necessary.

There is nothing new under the sun.

Ads, the internet, billboards, software sales, demand-side platforms, conversion tracking, it's all just the same old stuff.

Digital marketing is just the latest iteration of a vendor hawking his wares in an ancient market. It just happens to take place on the internet, rather than a sunny, crowded street in ancient Greece.

Not everyone has the natural gift of a storyteller, but it's not a hard skill to develop. Some folks are captivating right out of the gate, but not everyone.

It's a fairly simple process to become better at storytelling, and thus better at marketing and selling. You simply have to think about what makes a *bad* storyteller, and then avoid those behaviors.

We've all been in the presence of a bad storyteller. Everything that grates on your nerves as the recipient of a bad story is something broken about bad marketing. Think of someone who doesn't know when to shut up, but meanders on and on. Think of someone who is too fixated on small irrelevant details, so the plot never goes anywhere. Think of someone who doesn't clearly describe the setting or characters, so you can never really get proper context. Think of someone who feels like they're making it up. Think of someone who has no sense of humor.

Good marketing is good storytelling; be clear, concise, relatable, funny, true, and authentic. It's really as simple as that.

There is no such thing as making your marketing better with a "hook" or an "offer". There is no such thing as making sales better with "scripts" or "flows". This is just how people make up for a bad story. The world of infomercials and spam emails, of irresistible offers and gimmicky pitches, is just a temporary patch on a leaky tale.

Have a good story, and everything else just flows with it. You don't even have to pitch or hard-sell. You tell the story of what you have, and as long as you're not faking it, your marketing and sales will fall right into place.

## Chapter 12 Summary

*At the end of the day, marketing is storytelling: selling things through anecdotes. Your "brand", whether it's your own personal brand or a company's brand, is essentially a synonym for reputation. It's a long-term strategy. It may be difficult and even expensive to build over time, without any immediate attributable profit, but it pays dividends in the future. Those who are brave and forward-thinking enough to invest significant time and energy and money into building influence and reputation now will reap these rewards. It's a tough threshold, but this barrier to entry means that you will easily break out of the curve. Nobody else will be patient enough.*

# Chapter 13: Personality

Likability gets you hired.

A friend of mine was looking for a job, going through the standard rigmarole of interviews, screenings, recruiters, and rejections. At one point, he voiced an opinion that struck me violently: "there's only so much you can personally vibe with another professional."

It struck me so violently because I so strongly disagreed with the emotion. Of *course* you can vibe with other professionals: and not only vibe, but develop lasting friendships and fruitful relationships.

In thinking about the past few years of running our agency, I can see a constant stream of very real personal relationships that have developed out of what were initially business transactions (in all fairness, some of this is because I default towards fostering business transactions with individuals that I actually *like*).

We have traveled to see clients, bought a few rounds of beers for lunch, traveled to see competitors, mailed bottles of wine, held our business retreats in Greece and Egypt with all spouses and children included, kept casual email chats going back-and-forth for years, and any number of other non-business-appropriate things.

There seems to be a common assumption that business should be separate from relationships — that there can be no crossover between work hours and off hours.

That works in the corporate world, and it works in a strict German-style technocracy where you may not even know your colleague's first name, but it doesn't work in the sort of flexible, independent lifestyle that attracts modern entrepreneurs. The assumption seems to be that work is bad, and you shouldn't want to include it in the rest of your life.

In my mind, work is awesome, and it's an integral part of my life because I have fun doing it. I haven't always had fun at work. Ironically enough, it takes a lot of work to start to enjoy work. The results are worth the trouble.

There are very real tangible benefits to liking the people you work with.

Say that two of your colleagues are struggling in their positions. One is a buddy you get along with well: you like the same things, he brings donuts into the office, sometimes you grab a few drinks with him after work, once he helped you move some heavy furniture at home. The other colleague is a loner, someone who never showed up to a happy hour or engaged in polite conversation, someone who never refilled the coffee machine and who left his empty Doritos bag open on the break room counter. When a crisis emerges — as is the norm in all companies — which one of these guys are you going to go out of your way to help out?

The answer is as obvious as the question, but for some reason some folks find it uncomfortable because it implies that mere job performance, credentials, seniority, or technical qualifications are not enough to thrive in a career. You also have to be nice.

Here's the rub: it's pretty easy to get qualifications and credentials. It's not difficult to sign up to get an MBA on the weekends. But it's pretty damn hard to change your personality, and turn yourself from a sour loner into a pleasant team player.

Anybody can sign up for a program to append BA, PMP, PMI-RMP, MBA to their LinkedIn profile.

Not everybody can become the cool guy, although it would be far more valuable for their own career if they did.

The work doesn't matter as much as *who* does it. It's a fact which doesn't sit well with some, especially when we're talking about service businesses. People buy based upon your *likability* — not whether you're the absolute world's best practitioner, or whether you're the cheapest.

At first glance, this seems unfair. After having this discussion with a few folks, I've realized that many more people disagree with this statement than I first suspected. Because, if all things were equal, shouldn't someone hire for value — getting the best work for the money?

Yes, if all else is equal.

But things are *not* all equal. And there is a hidden, intangible value to relationships that often trumps specifications.

Let's take an example. A midsize e-commerce brand is looking for a marketing agency to help them run their ad campaigns. Perhaps they find a few potential agencies, do some research, and set up meetings. If things go as they typically do, the brand will quickly filter out the "under-performers" (agencies which can't deliver, or don't have the technical capacity) and end up with a couple solid choices. There are lots of agencies out there who *do* have solid technical skills.

So it comes down to the last two quality contenders. What factor is going to break the stalemate?

It's how much the decision-maker at the brand actually likes the personality of the marketing agencies that they're talking to.

Seems unfair, right?

Your personality shouldn't affect the quality of your work, right? Who cares whether you're super likable or not, as long as you get the work done? But at this point the work quality is irrelevant — there is always someone better, and there is always someone cheaper. Fortunately for the vast majority of us, who aren't always the world champion and also aren't always the cheapest, all things else aren't equal.[26]

The intangible advantage of personality is trust.

---

[26] *If you do think you're the world's best, you're delusional. There are approximately eight billion other people out there. Why don't you just settle for the top one percent in your field?*

Trust is a complex social factor that every human develops over the course of a life. We start to see patterns, remember past behaviors, develop a sixth sense, and eventually learn to spot trustworthy people (and usually, we like these sorts of people).

Hiring a company or person you trust (and *like*) is critical because it's insulation against problems down the road. Jiving with someone is critical because you understand how they think, and they understand you. Sharing things in common means you can develop an initial social interaction into a lasting relationship, and it suddenly becomes much easier to get anything done. You have support when you need it, and you will gladly give support when they need it.

Marketing and sales can seem very tangible on the surface, but that feeling is the least important part. The most important part is what's under the surface: the relationships and trust and brand and authority. The social lubrication that allows things to happen.

An engine can be perfectly functional. But try to run it without oil, and it burns up within a few minutes.

That's the power of likability.

Talk to your average marketer, especially those working in-house or at large ad agencies, and perhaps nothing is hated more universally than the sales people.

It's quite a short-sighted and uninformed position, because the reality is that marketing *is* sales. Marketers just tend to have a bit of an intellectual flair and creative vanity. It's tempting to put a barrier down between us, the marketers, and those people, the sales guys.

At the end of the day, we're all trying to get stuff sold. So what's the difference? We're all on the same transactional spectrum. We're either selling services or products. The marketers don't get paid if the sales guys don't get paid. The money comes from somewhere, and that somewhere is the folks we're selling to.

Many marketers have a knee-jerk reaction to this, and they'll pitch you a colorful story about brand development and client-focused messaging and ideal customer personas and solving problems for the public. For some reason, many marketing professionals, especially the most abstracted of them, have an allergy to commercializing their profession. I'm afraid, however, that they'll only find themselves in the deep waters of cognitive dissonance if they don't boil marketing down to its simplest concept. There may be a time and a place for anti-capitalism, but marketing sure isn't the place.[27]

Sales gets a bad rap because many people do sales very, very poorly. When people think of bad salesmen, that's because bad salesmen are doing sales badly. And when the sales people are doing sales badly, marketing is going to do marketing badly. Don't let people who practice either sales or marketing poorly influence your perception of the discipline as a whole. You want to lean into good marketing and good sales.

---

[27] *If you don't love capitalism, do both yourself and your clients a favor and get out of marketing or sales.*

I'm good at sales — it took me a while to discover this, and eventually even admit this, because for many years I retained an allergy to the idea of sales. But what I also discovered is that I was naturally good at soft sales (almost a sort of anti-sales) and it wasn't really that different than marketing and branding and advertising in general.

*Good* marketing is not *hard* marketing. It's soft marketing. And the best sales method is also the soft sales method.

If you've found yourself allergic to the idea of hard sales, then you need to embrace the idea of soft sales. If the thought of cold calling, door knocking, cold emailing, spamming people on LinkedIn, or plastering your face on billboards makes your skin crawl, then you will absolutely love the practice of soft sales.

Soft sales means developing relationships, befriending folks, buying them drinks, hanging out with groups you like, contributing to the industry, writing books, speaking at conferences, doing audits or small consulting calls, joining small groups, helping new folks in the industry, taking clients out to eat, or generally just being an interesting person that folks like to work with.

At no point in nearly eight years of co-running an agency, have I ever handed someone a business card, pitched for an RFP, cold-called anyone, sent a cold email, or knocked on a single door. (To be clear, I'm not saying these things are bad, I'm just saying I've never had to do them).

Instead, I've just done a lot of up-front work which eventually results in passive inbound leads for our agency: posting on Twitter, publishing technical marketing books, attending conferences, joining competitors for dinner, buying clients a round of drinks, doing free audits and consults, speaking at events or joining podcasts as a guest, and a litany of other work.

But more than anything, what has resulted in great success for our agency is developing the brand — both personal and professional — that convinces people they want to work with us, before I've even met them.[28]

When someone submits a form, sends an email, or gives me a call, I don't have to convince them they need to work with us. They already want to. They almost already know me, because they've read stuff I've published. So as a result, I've actually had to convince people we're *not* the right fit far more often than convincing people we *are* the right fit.

---

## Chapter 13 Summary

*When it comes to sales, the most common approach is the worst approach. The hard-selling, boiler room, cold-calling outbound approach is low-effort. The only barrier to entry for the "hard sales"*

---

[28] *Another lesson I learned over time was that "faking" your personality gets you nowhere. You have to be who you are, even if you think parts of that personality might not be popular or political correct or even entirely professional. You can and should always improve yourself, of course, but you can't fake your interests. It's annoying. People can tell.*

*approach is access to either an email account or a phone number, so you're competing with a lot of burnt-out salesmen who outcompete by the sheer amount of numbers dialed. It is more sustainable, more reputable, and more lucrative at the end of the day to instead focus on your own likability, familiarity, and reputation. People will come to you, rather than you having to go to them. This makes everything easier, smoother, and more satisfactory in the long run.*

# Chapter 14: Do People Change?

My mother-in-law still does not know that Anya and I visited Chernobyl a few years ago. She would not understand. I understand *why* she would not understand: like any good mother, her child's health is of utmost importance, and a radioactive Exclusion Zone is just not something that most mothers would be comfortable with.

Visiting Chernobyl was one of the coolest things I ever scratched off my bucket list. Like any nerd, I'd played my share of *Stalker* during my teenage years, and seeing the Ferris wheel, and the radar array, walking up abandoned apartment buildings, seeing empty Olympic-sized pools, and throwing bits of biscuits to oversized eight-foot-long catfish roiling in the cooling canals was everything I'd waited for.

Access to Chernobyl is tightly controlled. The Exclusion Zone is a roughly 1,000 square mile area around the reactor, surrounded by razor wire fence and guarded by military. Upon exiting the Zone, you must clean your shoe soles and walk through a Geiger counter to ensure you don't track radiation out into the real world.

What I did not know, until we actually entered the Zone, is that there still exist people who are called "self-settlers". These are mostly little old ladies who, almost four decades later, refuse to leave their homes. They were forcefully removed several times, but they kept finding ways to return to their homes.

These self-settlers still live in the Zone, farming in their gardens, trading vegetables for cigarettes with the various workers who come into the Zone in shifts to operate the reactor containment area (in case you didn't know, the melted-down reactor is entombed in a massive concrete sarcophagus).

Can you imagine not wanting to leave?[29] And not wanting to leave enough that you keep going back, even when forcibly removed? Isn't that crazy?

It actually doesn't really surprise me, because people are so extremely resistant to change.

If humans are truly as brittle and unchanging as this theory indicates, then this should inform our tactics when we're marketing something or selling something.

I have often wondered at the typical marketing "stack" which usually includes some form of convincing or mind-changing. Equally, I've wondered at the typical sales slop that's regurgitated in sales conferences and business books, the process of hammering someone on the head with a sales hammer until they pay you money.

Here's why: it *actually doesn't work.*

---

[29] *Can you imagine trading cigarettes for radioactive vegetables?*

I have talked to countless business owners who take a high volume, hard sales, megaphone-style approach to drumming up business. These owners are working very hard on making their lives needlessly painful. When you depend upon volume, you are faced with high amounts of possible churn, an immediate drop off of new business once your prospecting efforts stop, and extremely high expense ratios. And after all of that filling-up-the-lead-bucket, you're *still* having to convince each of those prospects to become a customer.

And since people don't like to change, you've created an uphill battle for yourself. Wouldn't it have been far easier to develop a trickle of very interested people who already want to work with you?

A few times a year, I meet with other marketers, sometimes in random cities across the world, sometimes for conferences, sometimes at events thrown by clients. Other agency owners, freelancers, consultants, in-house talent, and marketers of all stripes gather on the peripheries of these sorts events to grab drinks and swap stories.

There is some technical talk, to be sure, but what an outsider or newcomer might not expect is just how little the technical talk matters among these folks. In many ways, these people are at the very top of their game — the most skilled and successful people in their respective specialties. The technical stuff matters, of course, but that's actually not the most important aspect of meeting up with industry experts.

The most important thing is developing relationships. That seems like a shallow feel-good thing to say, but I can't believe it more strongly.

Osmosis is a very real thing. The saying "you become who your five closest friends are" is relevant. These folks are soaking up experience from their colleagues.

Every mistake that could be made has been made by these people. They're not perfect! But the beauty is that every one of the others who listens to their warnings and nightmare stories learns from them, and hopefully if we learn from the mistakes of others we won't have to suffer the same consequences.

Equally, the wins are also shared — there is rarely room for secrets in such a space. Tactics, strategies, and ideas are passed back and forth, and everyone leaves knowing a bit more about what works in today's marketing arena.

Do you know what is perhaps most interesting about this elite group of authors, speakers, agency owners, and marketers at huge brands? It's not just that they're amazing at their craft (although most are). They are good, but there are millions of marketers out there, and plenty of them are technically better at many things. It's mostly that they're great at connecting with others. Combine likability and frankness and communication with actual technical skills, and you end up with two perfectly complementing hemispheres of abilities.

You don't have to be the world's most charming speaker, or the world's most beautiful person, or the world's most charismatic communicator. You really just have to be friendly.

And this, boiled down, is the power of soft skills.

Marketing is fantastic. Technical abilities are crucial.

But as I am fond of saying, the difference between a skilled unpleasant marketer and a skilled pleasant marketer is about $100,000.

## Chapter 14 Summary

*People are inflexible. It is hard to convince people to change. It simply inefficient to brow-beat your customers into accepting an upsell. It's not what's best for them, and it's not better for you in the long run. It is better, then, to establish your brand as an authority. The sales will sell themselves.*

# Chapter 15: Standing Out In A Sea of Gatekeepers

People are not truly creative.

C.S. Lewis once wrote something along the lines of "man can not create a truly new monster". What he meant by this is that humans are really only good at combining old things in new ways. It's very difficult, if not impossible, to come up with an entirely new idea that isn't drawn from something else you've experienced. A dragon, after all, is just a lizard with some fire and wings.

That's why any difference, any change, any slight slant in trajectory at all, can break the "system" in a major way you can easily take advantage of.

The marketing industry is like every other industry: a lot of old players, a lot of young upstarts, a lot of walled gardens, and a lot of blue oceans ready to be explored.

The old players in marketing are the big ad agencies: the massive holding companies worth billions of dollars and running some of the world's largest campaigns. They're powerhouses, to be sure, but that doesn't mean they're invincible. As a matter of fact, their sheer size is their own Achilles heel: they're often inefficient, a bit outdated, a drudgery to work at, and have a hard time retaining talent for too long. Although they pay well, they don't pay *ridiculously* well.

The young upstarts can run the gamut from the clever and ambitious, to the confused and confusing grifters and scam artists that unfortunately plague the industry. On one end, you can have some of the most ambitious, hard-working, and intelligent young marketers in the world making things and doing good work, and on the other hand you can have some of the most irresponsible folks who have very little experience doing actual marketing work, and a lot of experience selling "the dream", which usually involves selling courses or masterminds or ethically questionable funnels of morally questionable products.

Walled gardens can include agencies themselves, but the most challenging walled gardens in marketing actually are the communities of experts in any given niche. Unfortunately, the longer folks are in a niche, the more they are incentivized to keep new people out of it. Clearly this approach doesn't sit well with me (which is why I like to write these books to help folks get into marketing!) but it doesn't change the fact that it can be very, very challenging to break into a specific community. It's just a case of the old guard falling behind in their tactics and strategy, and instead of staying relevant, they find that it's easier to just keep new folks out. I don't like this. It's lazy, and bad for the industry. My sincere recommendation is to ignore these folks (who are thankfully few and far between) and just keep plunging ahead. You do not need their permission to work in their industry.

The blue oceans ready to be explored are numerous. I can't even name them; if I were able to, they wouldn't be that new. The possibilities in marketing are endless, and ever-changing. Finding these new technologies, industry verticals, acquisition strategies, and different approaches is what gives new marketers an edge over the old folks.

You know the stereotype of the golf buddies, the country club members, the fraternity brothers, shaking hands and working things out? It's the good-old-boy stereotype, a sort of you-scratch-my-back-and-I'll-scratch-yours. It gets a lot of flak.

But guess what: it works, and it works for a reason.

You don't have to like it, but personal relationships are the oil through which the business world gets things done. This level of personal trust and handshake business is uniquely American, but it's filtering slowly throughout the rest of the world. And I'll just have to say, it's a good thing.

Here's why it works.

Put yourself in the position of someone running a big project. Say that you've got a $10 million project that's in the pipeline. It's a lot of money from the investors, a lot of time and energy from the stakeholders, and the future of the entire business depends upon it.

As with any process, you're likely considering many different vendors to help push this project through to completion.

Of course every vendor thinks they can do it. Every one of them will make a promise. Those promises will likely even be legally binding. But legally binding doesn't mean a thing in the world of business, because even if all the evidence is on your side, who are you going to collect from? If something goes wrong, your business project has failed and you likely have a bankrupt vendor at fault. But you, the showrunner, bear the brunt of that responsibility.

This is where the handshake golf-club apparatus comes into play. Detractors like to call this nepotism or favoritism, but in reality I think it's just safety. Of course you would prefer to hire someone you know and respect: who wouldn't? Of course you'll default towards the proven, safe bet: only a fool wouldn't.

The only people who don't like this approach are the outsiders, because they're not in the club.

I understand this, because for years and years I wasn't in the club. I was always the outsider, and I always wondered how in the world we could land these big projects, big clients, big budgets. I kept trying to figure out how to become an insider, and to be honest it probably took a decade in marketing before I even had a hint of how it happened.

As it turns out, you have to let them come to you. If you knock on their door, you won't get an answer. Those in the know — or in other words the country club people — are not unintelligent folks, and they gate-keep access to their world very strictly. People are always trying to get into that club, but it's invite-only.

Becoming an expert is the way that you find yourself slowly gaining access to this circle. Developing trust via domain authority, and freely helping out those who inquire, gives you a sort of karma that builds up over time. And eventually you're invited in.

Have you ever noticed that whenever an industry starts slipping, the tactics get desperate?

Whenever something stops working so well, and the former experts are starting to get gray around the temples, there is usually a last-ditch grab for control.

The term "Luddite" comes from the followers of Ned Ludd in the early 1800s, who would sabotage machinery in textile mills, brickworks, and other factories. Suddenly, weaving things by hand wasn't competitive anymore, and they were seeing their careers go down the drain.[30]

I've seen this happen in countless situations. It happened when photography went from film to digital. It happened when barbers became fancy. And now, it's even starting to happen with online marketing, and search marketing to be specific.

Here's how it plays out in real life.

Old-school barbers had their heyday. For decades, barbers cut

---

[30] Conniff, Richard. "What the Luddites Really Fought Against." Smithsonian, Smithsonian.com, 2011

simple haircuts for $5. Then, hipster hairstylists, the kind of guys with leather aprons who wax their moustaches, came around and started charging $60 for a fancy cut. And people paid it. Suddenly, the old barbershops were left with geriatric customers, still operating in terms of 1970 dollars.

So what do the old barbers do? Well, they sure don't learn how to cut a new haircut. They just start lobbying and enforcing haircutting laws (yes, haircutting laws are a thing). They call in anonymous tips to the state haircut police (yes, this is also a thing) for serious violations like trimming sideburns with the wrong type of hair license (yes, this is also another thing).

Old-school photographers rode a gravy train all the way through the 1990s. They had expensive cameras, expensive film, expensive processing, and expensive studios.

High barrier to entry. Not much competition.

That's why there used to be portrait studio storefronts located in every courthouse square in every small town across America.

They're all closed (or closing) now.

Digital SLRs came around, and for $750 you have a camera that's arguably better than the $25,000 film setup that those portrait studios were using. A new vein of photographers, no longer priced out of an industry, commoditized the market. How many average families need Ansel Adams to come take graduation photos, anyway? So what do the old film photographers do?

I know what they did, because I was just dipping my toes into photojournalism right about the time the last rolls of Kodachrome were kicked into the mausoleum. I graduated from college in 2011, and went straight into media production.

The old boys refused to cut their rates to meet market demand, and so they started bleeding clients. They spent their newly found free time hopping onto message boards and ridiculing industry newcomers in ALL-CAPS. They dismissed digital cameras, didn't help the younger tribe enter the profession, started charging convoluted licensing fees for ongoing usage, and even sued people for reprinting their family photos without permission!

It was a very cutthroat time. I mean, for something as innocent as photography, it was ridiculous. The old school boys even threatened to bring lawsuits towards new videographers who said they "filmed things" — ostensibly, this lawsuit was justified because film stock is technically a substrate of silver emulsion, not a digital file. These guys were crazy. They held onto the mast of their sinking ship and drowned.

Now, the first wave of online marketers (the ones who jumped into a burgeoning bull market in the late 1990s and early 2000s) are beginning to do the same thing. Online marketing twenty or thirty years ago was an entirely different world. You could charge five figures for building a simple HTML website.[31] You could throw up a banner ad and make a thousand sales in your first week. Now, things have changed.

---

[31] *This is exactly how I paid rent for a decade.*

There are millions of ad agencies and marketers — the entire world is competing with you.

The old boys haven't put in the effort to keep up with the current tactics, and are instead falling back to regulations and credentials. They try to create certifications, industry associations, write bitter diatribes on forums, diss successful young marketers...and meanwhile haven't updated their skillset since June 2006.

One of the latest trends in my world are a bunch of old farts who created an industry association, are trying to develop a certification, and are now encouraging the adoption of government regulations so people need to get a license in order to advertise online. They even want to enforce their ancient industry pricing models, preventing new agencies from experimenting with cheaper or more flexible payment options.

The only reason these guys are saying this is because they've lost the pace. They aren't bringing actual value to their clients, they aren't updating their pricing structure, and their retainers are getting dropped.

This walled-garden, enforce-playground-rules approach to success is distasteful to me. It's distasteful for anyone who wasn't already in the "in crowd", anyone who is trying to break into a new discipline.

I don't have a problem with protecting your livelihood (we should all be able to do whatever we want, as long as it doesn't hurt someone else) but creating and enforcing new playground rules is distasteful because it reeks of desperation.

If you're doing well, you won't have to protect your revenue by shutting others out. Times change, and sometimes you have to change with the times.

The problem with gatekeeping certain industries (or gatekeeping certain areas of expertise, for that matter) is that it reduces the spread of knowledge.

It means that some knowledge is limited to a certain class or profession. And, as is often quipped, knowledge is power. It also is anti-scientific: by definition, shouldn't theories and hypotheses be defended?

The free market of ideas is extremely important for growth, for innovation, for exploration, and for discovery. If we create artificial walls that block out new ideas, there is no expansion of knowledge that is happening. The old blood becomes stagnate: the new blood is prevented from access to the resources needed to develop new wisdom.

Preventing the common man (perhaps those who don't have certain degrees, or certifications, or ad industry heritage) from becoming too curious about domains of knowledge is a form of elitism at the highest. At the worst, it causes bad information to fester. No one is always one hundred percent correct, after all, and bad information needs to be challenged.

Going into sales or marketing, you should be aware of the status quo, and that established players will often try to erect moats to keep the new folks out.

My advice: ignore them, plunge forward, and create your new club!

---

## Chapter 15 Summary

*Being unorthodox in any given industry means that you may attract the wrath of the established players: the gatekeepers who won't like you changing the rules. For example, in running our agency, one of my favorite tactics is providing huge amounts of free advice and actual tactical tips — without asking for a single dime. Discosloth has gotten actual pushback from gatekeepers within the digital advertising industry, because it negatively reflects upon their business model (many agencies charge for discovery, or audits, or strategic tips). I will happily subvert the gatekeepers here: the proof is in the pudding. Do not worry about industry best practices. As long as you're doing what works for you, double down on it. Infuriate the dinosaurs.*

# Chapter 16: Time Horizon & Delayed Gratification

In 1972, a professor at Stanford named Walter Mischel conducted a famous study which would become known as the "Stanford marshmallow experiment". [32]

Children were left in a room for 15 minutes with a single marshmallow, and offered the choice of either one immediate reward, or two later rewards (as long as they didn't eat the marshmallow by the time the researcher returned). If they were able to resist eating the single marshmallow, they were rewarded with another snack of their choice.

The beauty of this study was not quite so much the insight about kids and marshmallows, but that it was a quite extensive study that actually followed up on the child's progression through life for years.

It turned out that the children with delayed gratification (those who were able to hold out for 15 minutes for an extra reward) were distinctly more successful in life. Children with delayed gratification

---

[32] Mischel, Walter, and Ebbe B. Ebbesen. "Attention in Delay of Gratification." Journal of Personality and Social Psychology

had higher SAT scores, completed better degrees, had lower BMI, and in general had a more fully developed prefrontal cortex.

What is most interesting to me are the reasons *why* these children had better delayed gratification. The researchers were curious about this as well, and as it turns out, the children's familial background had a significant part to play in how patient and "forward thinking" the children were. Children with stable families (non-divorced parents, higher income) scored far better than children from unstable families (divorced parents, lower income).

In general, follow-up studies reinforced the results of the original Mischel study, and expanded on the results by showing that often differences in culture played an even greater part in how a child would turn out in terms of life accomplishments.

The important takeaway about delayed gratification is not that it is bad to get something now. It is that sacrificing current desires in order to achieve even greater desires in the future is hard, but well worth it.

We have a difficult time thinking about the future because it is abstracted. It is very easy to think about what you need to do today, because your needs today are very obvious (I am hungry now, I am poor now). It is very difficult to fast-forward several years into the future and consider what your needs may be (I may be hungry, I may be poor) — even more so if you take unknowns into consideration (I may have more mouths to feed, I may not be able to work in manual labor, the dollar may be inflated, my pension may not be there).

How does this apply to building business?

I co-run a small PPC agency. We run digital ads for mid-size and enterprise companies. We have a very simple service-based business model. A company wants to sell more widgets, so they pay us to run ads. We sell more widgets. Repeat cycle.

I often talk to fellow agency owners. To be honest, I know within a few moments if this owner is going to succeed, or if he is going to fail. There are a half-dozen instant signals (one of those is if they showed up to the meeting on time).

But the signal that is more important than any other — what time horizon is this person worried about? (At the very beginning there are always a lot of little short-term questions. I'm talking about strategy, big decision-making approaches).

The short-term statements are things like this:

—*I need to make $50,000 within 30 days*
—*I've got an offer that no client can refuse*
—*I know my worth, I have to charge more than that*
—*I want to work in a glamorous luxury niche*

The long-term statements are things like this:

—*I'm trying to hire better employees*
—*I need to reduce client churn*
—*How do I start increasing my fees?*

*—How much of a buffer do I need in the bank account?*
*—I want to reach $X annual profit in 5 years*

So often, I see agency owners worrying about this week, when they really should be worrying about next year or even what happens in 2028?

Of course there are emergencies, and sometimes this week really *does* need some attention.

But: if you had been thinking about this week five years ago, we probably wouldn't be having this discussion.

Preemptive beats reactive every single time.

Nothing has killed success in business faster than short-term thinking, and this is played out in marketing more visibly than almost anything else.

When prospects come to us with help on an advertising campaign, there are a litany of red flags I'm always keeping an eye out for. One of these is timeframe.

It's fine to want fast results (who doesn't?) but there is a specific species of advertiser who only wants fast results, and not only wants them, but is *dependent* upon fast results. This usually ends up being a company with extreme cash flow problems, which is never a recipe for success.

These cash flow problems are almost always the result of short-term thinking in the past: nothing compounds more efficiency than a series of bad decisions. Either they had cut corners early on, they picked a strategy that was conducive to immediate results rather than long-term stability, or they are simply pulling the trigger on every single target opportunity that presents itself, without a thought in the world for how this shot could affect the business later on.

Digital marketing is especially prone to these sorts of issues since so much of it happens so fast. Give any paid search monkey a million dollar budget, and they can spend it in a single day. Doesn't mean it's the *smart* way to do it, but it can be done.

A marketer must mitigate this tendency towards short-term thinking, and instead focus on what is best. Sometimes, that's quick, fast experiments or one-off campaigns. Other times, it's a years-long strategy of building a brand and fostering community around a concept. Almost always, it's a combination of the two: making things profitable now, but also ensuring that you're working towards even greater profitability next year.

One of the easiest ways to make better decisions is to stretch out your time horizon.

If immediacy is your primary goal, then long-term success is going to evade your grasp. It's fine to want quick results, but quick results as the end-all goal will curtail your success on a longer time horizon.

And a longer time horizon *should* be your priority, unless you're already eighty-five years old, in which case you should have taken care of the details long ago.

We've all been in dire straits, but unless you're staring your coffin in the face, needing immediate results is an indication of other problems.

If you're building a strategy out of desperation, it's too late. You're simply bandaging poor decisions, not creating something new. You're being reactive, not proactive.

So think further. Not three months, not even three years, but 15 years in the future. Of course little things need to be taken care of today, but really *anything* worth doing will have second- and third-order effects far into the future.

If you are thinking through something (figuring out how to sell a software, creating a branding campaign, determining a pricing model, wondering what to eat for lunch) then you at least need to *think* about thinking for the future.

Keeping the future as a sort of abstract presence in the back of your mind, even if it doesn't directly influence your daily decisions, does help put small things into larger perspective. Every one of those small decisions compounds. Eating fast food for lunch one time will not make an iota of difference in your health 15 years from now, but if you eat fast food for lunch daily, you will almost certainly reap the consequences. The same goes for little business decisions.

I see this often in agencies or consultants who nickel-and-dime their clients. They charge for *everything*. They track every 15 minutes. They charge for hopping on a phone call. There's no concept of "no strings attached" — literally everything they do is transactional and quantified.

Folks who do this will likely make a little bit more money *now*, but they will almost certainly make less money over the next 15 years.

---

## Chapter 16 Summary

*A longer time horizon which informs your decision-making and tactics is always better — in the long run. Short-term pain nearly always results in long-term gain. Apparently, humans are naturally impatient, and as the Stanford marshmallow experiment showed, children who have stronger impulse control turn out to be more successful later in life. This is echoed directly in any brand's approach to sales and marketing. It's always tempting to prioritize results now (and of course, we all have to eat this week, not next year) but the longer intro the future you can position your goals, the more successful your efforts will become.*

# UNORTHODOXY

# End Times

# UNORTHODOXY

# Chapter 17: Tabula Rasa

The Nordic myth of Ragnarök is in many ways similar to the end-time stories of other cultures, and even bears striking similarities to both the Christian eschatology of death and rebirth, and the creation story of the Garden of Eden. Some elements of this Nordic myth are perhaps most familiar to the modern reader by being deeply embedded into Tolkien's *Silmarillion*.

The idea of Ragnarök, which means "twilight of the gods" in Old Norse, is that a series of apocalyptic events destroy the current world and reshape the cosmos.

In the myth of Ragnarök, as told in both the poetic and prose *Eddas*, the end of the world is triggered by the wolf Fenrir breaking loose from his chains and devouring the sun. Many gods die battling their enemies, including Odin, Thor, and Loki.

The world is engulfed in flames and a new world emerges from the ashes. Two humans — Lif and Lifthrasir — survive by hiding in the World Tree, and proceed forth to repopulate the world.

At some point in every industry, there is a Ragnarök. It is a time where everything that exists is flipped upside down. The tables are turned. The old guard is ushered out, and the new guard marches in.

There will always be gatekeepers. In the world of marketing and advertising and sales, those might be the big ad agencies, or corporate holdouts, or dinosaurs who resist changing their *modus operandi* after four or five decades of doing it a certain way.

But gatekeeping is a way of *retaining* success, not *attaining* it.

If we—the marketers and advertisers and salesmen of the world —want to reach significant success in the future, it won't be reached by following the best practices of old. It'll be by forging ahead and trying out new ideas. It'll be through parsing the current status quo, and taking only the best ideas from the present. It'll be through discarding the bad ideas and bloated strategies of the past.

As I mentioned in the beginning of this book, nothing is truly new under the sun. At the end of the day, marketing is just selling things via stories. Everything else is just a costume thrown on top.

And as I have also alluded throughout the book, bell curves aren't deceptive, especially when it comes to skills and outcomes in tech-adjacent pursuits like digital advertising or software sales or internet marketing. They are not a gentle, symmetrical curve where most folks rest at an easy fifty percent. The barrier to entry is low, so there is a lot of clutter down at the very bottom, and a few very talented folks at the top who just "get it".

If you are one of the people who just get it, the probability of success isn't 50%. It's more like 90%.

It is merely a question of time in the game.

But—and this is a big qualifier—you do have to *get it.*

At some point you will find yourself (or your agency, or your ecommerce business, or whatever else you're running) at a critical inflection point.

There are countless moments in a career or project where you can choose diverging paths. Some of these moments are more impactful than others.

Nearly everyone finds themselves a blank slate moment, a *tabula rasa*, a point in time at which you can change your current trajectory, a time in which it is especially easy to either build or destroy your future.

We all make wrong decisions.

But there are many inflection points, many decisions, many times where you can pivot, many times where you're faced with that *tabula rasa*, the blank slate from which you can reinvent that which is going wrong.

You can withstand one wrong decision. You can come back from two or three bad calls. Each decision may just be a very slight deflection off course. But statistically, if you're faced with a constant onslaught of inflection points and you make all the wrong calls, you'll find yourself going one hundred and eighty degrees in the wrong direction (contrarian in the worst sense of the word!) and at that point it's very unlikely you can undo all of those bad calls.

It is true that some businesses have had it worse than others.

And that is why I think we have to judge people based on where they started, and how much they have progressed…and less on where they happen to be right now.

To whom much is given, much will be required, and this is reflected directly in seeing which decisions people make in their careers or business pursuits. It is reflected directly in those inflection points—that constant barrage of decisions—and seeing what a person chooses to draw after their slate has been erased.

For the internet, it may be time for a Ragnarök: a rebirth of the cosmos!

# Afterword

If I were to boil this book down into a single line, it would be this: it actually *is* all or nothing.

It's important to not become mindlessly mainstream. You can't just go with the flow because it's easy. But at the same time, your path should be informed: not merely a knee-jerk reaction to the complete opposite of normal. You can't just be good, you've got to be great.

Much easier said than done.

In order to truly become unorthodox, you have to commit. There's no sitting on the fence. There's no Plan B. Hedging your bets, when it comes to truly breaking out of the mainstream, building a brand, marketing yourself, selling your services, and creating something *worth* creating is never really going to be satisfactory.

You've got to embrace the possibility of being unorthodox. You've got to go all-in.

# Book List

Here is a short list of books I've found enjoyable and informative. It's important to note that I don't only read books which I agree with 100%. It is important to read books that disagree or even contradict with my natural viewpoints, otherwise I'm just stuck in a silo.

### *Zero To One: Notes on Startups, or How to Build the Future,* Peter Thiel with Blake Masters

To date, one of the most unique books on mimetic theory and contrarianism and niching down that I've ever read. It's famous within the startup world for a reason. It will definitely challenge your assumptions. If I were to boil down this book into a single sentence, it would be: "why are you trying to compete when you could just… be so different you don't have to compete?"

### *Softwar: An Intimate Portrait of Larry Ellison and Oracle* by Matthew Symonds

Even if you just read the first few chapters, this is a very insightful book on how a very successful sales guy (Larry Ellison) does sales. Written in 2003, it's as relevant as ever. I do not have what it takes to build a multi-billion dollar company, but it's interesting learning from those who do.

### *The WEIRDest People In The World: How the West Became Psychologically Peculiar and Particularly Prosperous,* Joseph Henrich

A sort of macro history book which is a fascinating look at culture, and why we are the way we are. Henrich dives into the psychological evolution of societies and attempts to discern why WEIRD cultures (Western, Educated, Industrialized, Rich and Democratic) have such different behavioral patterns than other countries. It's a useful look at how consumers have different incentives and biases.

### *Stop The Scale: Building a Digital Agency You Actually Like* by Kirk Williams

I'm a big fan of how Kirk runs his agency. If you're a marketer type who's running an agency, it might be worth learning how he thinks.

*Becoming A Digital Marketer: Gaining the Hard & Soft Skills for a Tech-Driven Marketing Career* by Gil & Anya Gildner
*Building A Successful Micro-Agency: A Guide to Starting Profitable & Sustainable Digital Marketing Agencies* by Gil & Anya Gildner

Perhaps I'm biased (definitely am). But when I write about my experiences I do not hold anything back. These books are everything Anya and I know about marketing, advertising, sales, branding, work, running an agency, and business in general. If this book has been at all insightful, you may enjoy these as well.

Follow me to the following corners of the 'net:

x.com/gilgildner

www.gilgildner.com

www.discosloth.com

www.ingramcontent.com/pod-product-compliance
Lightning Source LLC
Chambersburg PA
CBHW071251050326
40690CB00011B/2345